AI

The Battle for Sanguis

Volume II

The Diaeta Assembly

By: C.M. James

This series is dedicated to the new generation who will one day become future leaders. You have within you something of great significance at this very moment. Begin to let it manifest today so that when the world is yours, you will make it better than ever before.

Copyright © 2024

C.M. James
In partnership with Speak with My Assistant, LLC
Published by Speak with My Assistant, LLC

All rights reserved

This book, or parts thereof, may not be reproduced in any form without permission.

Cover art created from the public domain.

This book is a work of fiction. The events described here are imaginary. The names, settings, places, and characters are fictitious and not intended to represent specific places or persons, living or dead. Any resemblance to actual events or persons is coincidental or used only from a creative perspective. Any references to countries, states, or cities are only used as settings for a fictional plot and are not to be taken literally.

Contents

Chapter 1: Puss-Lee 1
Chapter 2: Royal Blood-Stained Rocks 12
Chapter 3: A Slave to Science 16
Chapter 4: Dark and Lonely Room 21
Chapter 5: Caged Secrets 26
Chapter 6: A Taste of Fear 31
Chapter 7: Coincidences 37
Chapter 8: Plasmatic 42
Chapter 9: The Upyr Path 48
Chapter 10: Cueball Calathea 54
Chapter 11: Before The One, Comes One 60
Chapter 12: "Excuse Me, Did You Say Something?" 67
Chapter 13: Whispers of Rebellion 73
Chapter 14: A Series of Recurring Coincidences .. 79
Chapter 15: Azure's SLY Plan 84
Chapter 16: An Undead Meet & Greet 89
Chapter 17: Powers Revealed 98
Chapter 18: Breaking News! 104
About the Author 110

*Chap*ter 1: Puss-Lee

———— ◆•●•◆ ————

The deafening noises from the sirens pierced through the air, drowning out all other sounds. The officer emerged from his patrol car, his authoritative presence commanding attention. Onlookers slowed their cars to a crawl, their curiosity piqued. The officer's badge glinted in the night, a symbol of power and control. His crisp uniform and confident stride exuded an air of authority.

The flashing lights' vivid blue, red, and white hues danced wildly in the rearview mirror. And yet, amidst the commotion, the driver remained calm and collected, his steely gaze fixed on the approaching officer. His passenger, on the other hand, was a different story. His nerves were evident as he frantically searched the car, his eyes darting from one corner to the next, searching the car for anything that would bring attention.

As the officer stalked behind the sleek, black vehicle, he lightly tapped the back of the car's trunk. His hand hovered near his waist, ready to draw his weapon at a moment's notice. With a trained eye, he scanned the car's interior, his gaze lingering on the rear seat and floorboard. Sweat beaded on his forehead as he prepared for what could be a dangerous encounter. "Good evening, sir," he called out, his voice tense yet controlled. "Would you mind rolling your window down so you can hear me?" He stood by the driver's door, his muscles tense and ready for any sudden movements. The driver turned his head to look at the officer, his eyes cold and calculating.

Without a word, the driver raised his pointer finger, as if to tell the officer to wait a moment. He turned back to face the front; his gaze fixed on the road ahead. Filled with nervousness, the passenger glared at the driver in disbelief. "What in the world are you doing dude? Lower your window bro," he exclaimed, his voice tinged with fear. But the driver remained stoic, refusing to acknowledge the passenger's pleas. "Sir, did you hear me? Do you mind rolling your window down for a minute so I can talk to you," the officer asked again, his voice growing sterner. Still, the driver paid him no attention, his eyes darting back and forth between the road and the rearview mirror.

The officer's heart raced as he braced himself for whatever may come next. Multiple senses were on high alert, the sound of his own pounding heart, the smell of fear and tension in the air, and the sight of the driver's steely gaze. Growing increasingly restless, the officer leaned over and gently rapped on the window.

Finally, the driver turned to face the officer with a sly grin, the corners of his mouth twitching with amusement. He rolled down his window with a sense of nonchalance as if he had all the time in the world. "What?" he asked, his voice dripping with confidence. The officer's eyebrows furrowed in frustration. "Sir, could you not hear me asking you to roll down your window?" he inquired, his tone stern and authoritative. The driver chuckled and leaned back in his seat. "Oh, I heard you. But I was thinking about something else as I was being pulled over. I suddenly remembered I was due for an oil change, trying to recall the last time I had one done. That's when you walked up, touching my goddamn car! Also, I hate being interrupted while I'm trying to think. And let's face it, you're not exactly going anywhere," the driver retorted, his smirk growing wider. The passenger shook his head and sank back into his seat, his hand cradling his forehead.

"Take a moment to consider your oil later. For now, do you know why I stopped you?" the officer asked, his patience waning. The driver shrugged his shoulders, his eyes still laced with amusement. "No, it hadn't crossed my mind because I really don't give a fuck! As I mentioned, I had more pressing matters occupying my thoughts. But, since you're here, I suppose you're at liberty to inform me of why you did," he replied, his voice laced with sarcasm. The officer sighed, his frustration still growing. "Well, thank you for allowing me to do so. Did you know you have a back taillight out," he asked, his tone firm. The driver's eyes flickered to the back of the car and then over to the passenger before returning to the officer. "You know what, now that you mention it, I did! My neighbor informed me about a month or two ago. But I just never got around to replacing it. I never really felt like it. They make those things so damn bright now," he exclaimed, his voice dripping with indifference.

The officer's gaze then turned to the passenger. "So, where are you gentlemen headed this evening?" he asked, trying to make conversation. Before the passenger could answer, the driver interjected with a smug smile. "We're headed to the same place you're headed, officer! The only difference is, I'll be there much later than you," he quipped. "Sir, have you had anything to drink tonight," the officer asked as he stepped backward, reaching for the radio attached to his jacket. The driver shook his head, his tone laced with arrogance. "I don't drink, at least what you are referring to at least," he replied, his smirk growing wider. The passenger let out a sigh of frustration and slumped further down in his seat.

"I can see that you may have misunderstood the current situation. Let's make this clear. I ask a question and expect an immediate and direct response from you. Not a smart-ass reply! Now, do you mind handing me your license and registration? And also, do you care to explain what is in the back seat floorboard? What is Blood Hub," he inquired, his voice firm and commanding.

As the officer shined his blinding flashlight into the car, he reached out with a clammy hand, anticipating the driver's license. The driver then lowered his window completely, rotated his body towards the officer, and locked eyes with him. "How about this for a direct fucking answer," his voice dripped with venom, "If you do not take that motherfucking light off of me immediately, I will snatch it from your fat pig hands and shove it where the sun doesn't shine. I will leave its light on and stick it up your pig ass and then watch you squeal in agony like the glowing pig bitch that you are!"

The officer, shocked by the driver's chilling reply, slowly moved away from the car once more; his hand still lingering on his radio ready to call for backup if needed. "I will need you to step out of the car right now! And don't make me ask you again!" the officer commanded. But the driver, unphased by the officer's demands, made a few of his own. "Get your hands off that fucking radio right now and walk your ass back to this car," he barked, his eyes fixed on the officer with a deadly stare.

The officer halted, his hands falling to his side as he suddenly wore a vacant expression. He then began to walk back towards the car, his heart pounding in his chest. "Now, that's a good boy. Now, what is your stupid name officer," the driver sneered. "It's Officer Greely," he replied robotically. "Okay, Officer Greely! So, do you have any children," the driver asked staring directly into Officer Greely's eyes. "Yes, I do. I have a daughter," Officer Greeley responded awkwardly. "That's great, has she been vaccinated yet, Greeley," the driver asked; voice cold and calculated. "Yes, of course she has. I make sure she stays up to date on all her vaccinations," Officer Greeley answered, his voice trembling. "Well, good fucking job, Dad! See, you've almost answered your own question and solved a case. You wanted to know what is in those containers in the back seat, correct," the driver's eyes gleamed with malice. Officer Greeley stood there, his mind racing as he tried to make sense of the situation.

"Your daughter would be a great donor. I have quite a few empty containers left for her to donate. How about you hop in the car and let's all go and say hi to her? We can see if she would like to make a hugely generous donation to fill up some of those empty containers in the back seat. What do you say, Greeley," the driver asked, voice laced with evil intentions.

Just then the passenger leaned over and grabbed him by his arm. "Julian, Stop! What the fuck man," he exclaimed, his voice shaking with fear and disbelief. Without turning around, Julian, the driver kept his eyes on the officer, a cold determination in his gaze. "Well, my friend here doesn't think we have time to do all of that. But that's because he doesn't have a desire, nor a need, for the same things I do," Julian's voice was smooth and almost hypnotic drawing Officer Greeley in closer. "Well, to be blunt, I like the way blood fucking tastes! Especially the kind of blood donation your daughter would produce," Julian stated with a dramatic flourish, his eyes glinting with something sinister.

At that moment, with a smile directed at the officer, he gradually parted his lips to reveal two shiny sizeable fangs protruding from the top of his mouth that only the officer could see at that angle. Upon viewing this, Officer Greely froze in place, his mind struggled to process the unbelievable scene before him. "Listen, Greeley," Julian's voice became low and commanding. "Let's establish who's really in fucking charge here! Do you see this vehicle I'm currently occupying?" The officer slowly nodded his head, sweat pouring from his face and forehead. "You will no longer pull this car over nor will you repeat anything that happened here tonight, that's if you even remember. But, if you do, I promise you I will come and collect that special donation from your daughter and then show you exactly how much I enjoy it! That will be right before I collect a donation from you! And I will collect it with these!" Julian exclaimed as he showed off his menacing fangs once again.

Officer Greeley stood there, his mind reeling from Julian's words and the sight of his fangs, still unable to move. "Now, I need for you to oink for me, bitch!" Julian requested, his tone mocking and cruel. The officer, still under Julian's spell, began to produce a few high-pitched noises resembling a pig's snort. Julian began to laugh, his voice echoing with dark amusement as he turned to look at the passenger. "You hear this shit, Lee? He sounds like that little slut you and Blake were tag-teaming a while back!" Still in total shock, Lee, the passenger, just sat there, his mind struggling to make sense of the situation.

"Well, Greeley, I've become bored with you already. Go get in your little pig car, you've held us up long enough with your shenanigans," Julian commanded, waving dismissively as if swatting away a pesky insect. Greeley slowly turned and began to walk back to his patrol car. But before he could reach his vehicle, Julian had one more request. His voice low and menacing, he yelled out, "Fuck that! I'm not done with you Greeley," he yelled, his words cutting through the air like a knife. Greeley, who was already halfway to his car, stopped and turned back around. "Do you see that ditch right there," Julian asked as he gestured towards an expanse next to the street adorned with a steep slope-like chasm. Greeley reluctantly nodded his head. "When I pull off, count to 30. Then, start your car, and smash the gas as hard as you can driving right into it. Do you fucking understand me," Julian's voice rose in intensity, his words laced with fury. Greeley nodded, his eyes darting back and forth between Julian and the ditch. With a deep breath, he turned and walked back to his vehicle.

"Bro, what in the hell just happened," Lee asked, his voice filled with disbelief as he turned to Julian. "Please, tell me I'm high right now! I can't believe any of this shit!" Julian just smirked, his eyes glinting with mischief. "Did you just freaking hypnotize him or something? Because you have to be a goddamn hypnotist or something," Julian shrieked, his expression remaining one of astonishment, as though he hadn't blinked the entire time.

Julian remained quiet; his eyes fixed on the road ahead. He pressed the power button on the car stereo, filling the car with loud, pulsating music. "If you can really hypnotize people, how come you haven't hypnotized us any new pussy, bro," Lee asked, his voice filled with disappointment. "We could be banging different chicks every night dude. All you would have had to do was hypnotize them. You've been holding out." Julian chuckled; his eyes still focused on the road. "You mean to tell me that, right now, your main concern is getting laid? See, that's your problem right there, Puss Lee! I'm going to start calling you that! Puss Lee, since that's all you think about," Julian remarked as he shook his head in disapproval. "Oh, and why would I need to hypnotize the chicks you go after? That's why you go after them because they don't need convincing. They're already desperate as is."

Lee fell silent, his eyes widening in realization. Julian just grinned, his eyes sparkling with mischief as he began to pull back onto the road. "But man, that shit you said about his daughter and you drinking her blood was great. You almost had me believing it!" Lee's voice was filled with admiration and wonder. "I thought for sure we were going to jail. Your aunt Azure would be so fucking pissed bro!"

Abruptly, Julian slammed on the brakes, bringing the car to a screeching halt. He whipped his head towards Lee, his expression grave and stern. "Listen to me," he said, his voice low and deadly. "If you even think about mentioning any of this to her, I will make sure you suffer a fate worse than death!" Lee's heart raced as he quickly leaned back against the door, nodding his head in agreement. Julian's eyes bore into him, making it clear that he meant every word.

As the car pulled away, Lee sat back and buckled his seatbelt. He then glanced back over at Julian, trying to lighten the mood. "Man, Julian, your auntie has you more scared than the cop back there, huh," he joked. They both chuckled, but Julian's laugh was laced with a slight tinge of fear. "You have no idea," he admitted. "Where is she at anyways? I need you to hypnotize her for me, bro," Lee inquired jokingly. Julian glanced back over at him with a serious look.

Suddenly, a loud bang echoed throughout the car causing Lee to jolt up from his seat. "What the hell was that" he shouted, whipping around to look behind him. Julian, eyes still glued to the road, acted as if nothing had happened. As Lee continued to look out the back window, he saw what looked like a car wreck. That is until he remembered Julian's last request to the cop. He immediately turned back to Julian; his eyes widened with shock. "Are you fucking kidding me," he exclaimed. Julian's lips curved into a small grin, but his face remained stoic. "How in the hell did you convince him to actually drive into the fucking ditch dude? I've seen you do some weird creepy shit, but this tops the goddamn cake," Lee proclaimed. "Listen, after we drop off these packages, we are going to the strip club," Lee declared, "And you, my friend, are going to talk to every single stripper in there." Julian, focusing on the road, just rolled his eyes. "And if I tap you on the shoulder and point to a certain stripper, you better work your hypnosis magic dude. We're taking all of the strippers back to a room tonight," Lee continued with a mischievous glint in his eye. "Whatever you say Puss-Lee," Julian replied as they continued down the road.

Chapter 2: Royal Blood-Stained Rocks

——————— ❖●❖ ———————

There's a winding path leading to the heart of what is known as The Gilead Mountains. There you'll find a somewhat hidden land with forest and rolling hills that are nestled around the rocky mountain peaks. The Gilead Mountains tower above the land, their jagged peaks piercing the heavens like spears, while the outer forest land stretches far and dark. It stands as silent sentinels, their ancient presence cloaked in mist, darkness, and an air of mystery that sends shivers down the spine. The stories that clung to these mountains are as old as time itself, whispers carried on the wind, tales that have passed down through generations.

But one story, in particular, stands out amongst the rest, a story of a battle that took place in these very mountains. A battle between a king and his son, their relationship torn apart by greed, power, and an insatiable thirst for control. The son, a complex and conflicted character, struggled to find his place in a world ruled by his father's iron fist. As the battle raged on, in the heart of these forest mountains, the son met his end. His body, a mere vessel for the turmoil and pain that consumed him, was cast into the deepest pits of the unknown. And as his soul departed this world, the mountains seemed to whisper his name, their ancient voices still can be heard by some.

The Gilead Mountains are more than just a backdrop to this story, they are characters in their own right. Their rugged terrain, treacherous peaks, and ever-changing moods add an element of an eerie evil lurking. And as the wind howls through the valleys, and the mist swirls around the trees, the story of the king and his son continues to echo through the ages.

Even in present times, the tale of the monarch and his realm remains widely familiar. Cities, holy sites, and even conflicts continue to revolve around the monarch's past. Not a single living being is unfamiliar with his name, such is the widespread recognition of his kingdom and his symbol. Despite the king's polarizing mix of virtuous and morally questionable actions, he is hailed as the most exceptional ruler to ever grace the pages of history. His actions, both noble and controversial, have left a lasting impact on the world, shaping it in ways that cannot be ignored.

Subsequently, the young prince's existence has become but a mere whisper in the grand scheme of things, a forgotten footnote in the annals of history. His name, now mostly unknown to the masses, remains confined to the shadows, veiled in obscurity. His character was a tapestry of contradictions, a conundrum that even the most astute minds could not unravel. According to the stories, no one in the kingdom could rival the prince's striking looks. His flawless physique, from his toes to his head, was unparalleled and deserving of endless adoration. His locks on his head were described to be so lengthy that they bore down with a weight of five pounds. But other than looks, to a certain population, he embodies everything his father was not, with a power that even surpasses his father. To some, the prince wasn't just a mere mortal but was and still is the locksmith to immortality.

Nestled within these mountains lies a place known to some as the "Forest of Ephraim." In this very spot, the lifeless body of the king's beloved son was callously discarded, left to rot and decay. The ground beneath was stained crimson with the blood of royalty, a stark contrast to the lush surroundings he experienced throughout his life. In the distance, the howls of wolves were a fitting soundtrack to his demise as the piercing shriek of bats resounded from below.

After millennia have passed, the majestic peaks, the vast terrain, the eerie howls and screeches endure, yet something new has emerged on top of the royal blood-stained rocks. The vast expanse is an otherworldly, almost dark but mystical sight. It is a place that is both jaw-dropping and unsettling, with its intricate stone formations that seem to defy gravity as it reaches the sky. Each piece of stone is meticulously handcrafted with the most scrupulous attention to detail. It is almost as if the landscape itself is a living, breathing entity, each stone pulsing with its own energy and purpose. At the center of this landscape stands a towering edifice, a grand structure that seems to be a sacred sanctuary. Its imposing presence, both intimidating and alluring, beckons to all who lay eyes upon it, although very few have. Adorned with intricate carvings and symbols, the vast expanse and its central edifice hold a dark secret.

As the moon casts its pallid light upon the forbidding landscape, figures begin to emerge from the depths of the forest with cloaks billowing like the wings of a predatory bird. One after another, they approach the central structure and ascend stone steps that lead to a grand marble door entrance. With a subtle motion of one of their wrists, the doors slowly open, allowing access into the core of the unknown.

Inside, the air was thick with anticipation, a palpable tension that coiled like a serpent ready to strike. There sat twelve thrones of ebony rose-like specters from the cavernous chamber all circling an extravagant marble table. One by one, they slowly settled into their designated places, a few pulling back the hooded cloaks that adorned their heads. From various corners of the globe, a dozen individuals gathered; six males and six females. The diverse backgrounds and apparent differences in age and nationality hold little significance; the one unifying trait among them is their cold undead state - The Diaeta Assembly.

Chapter 3: A Slave to Science

AS the days stretched into weeks and the weeks into months, time had blurred into a relentless stream of research, isolation, and a looming sense of captivity. The once vibrant virologist now moved through her days with a cautious resignation, her every action dictated by the ominous presence of her captors. Her apartment, back home, once a sanctuary of scientific exploration, had become a distant memory. The weight of her captivity pressed down upon her.

Meanwhile, hundreds of miles away Gail's disappearance had not gone unnoticed. Her face graced the screens of television sets and the pages of newspapers, a haunting reminder of a life stolen. Friends and colleagues rallied in her absence, determined to uncover the truth behind her disappearance. But their efforts yielded little more than unanswered questions and whispered rumors. And so, Gail remained trapped in a limbo of her own making, her fate intertwined with forces beyond her control. As the world outside continued to search for her, her absence felt like a gaping void, a silent testament to the injustices that lurked in the shadows.

Though her surroundings were sterile and impersonal, Gail had begrudgingly adapted to her new reality. Her captors, the same powerful men who had orchestrated her abduction, now commanded her expertise in the pursuit of their clandestine agenda. Under their watchful gaze, she toiled tirelessly, her scientific prowess harnessed for purposes both noble and nefarious. Her days were consumed by the pursuit of knowledge that served a darker purpose.

The scientific research and experiments Gail conducted were shrouded in secrecy, her findings destined for military and governmental purposes straddled the line between progress and peril, their implications far-reaching and ethically murky. Gail grappled with the moral ambiguity of her work, torn between the desire to appease her captors and the gnawing guilt of betraying her principles.

Gail's sense of isolation was punctuated only by the presence of her faithful companion, Provolone. The loyal dog provided a flicker of warmth in the cold confines of her new reality. Her captors allowed her to keep Provolone as long as she did as she was told. Together, they navigated the heavily secured corridors of the facility, Provolone's presence a silent comfort amid the oppressive atmosphere.

Despite the passage of time, Gail's desire to return home burned fiercely within her. Thoughts of her family, their faces etched in her mind, served as a beacon of hope amidst the darkness. But the threat of reprisal loomed large, a constant reminder of the consequences of disobedience. To defy her captors meant risking not only her own life but the lives of those she held dear.

Gail was often the rebellious type; never fully content with following the rules and living a simple quiet life. But now she was forced to live in a small, cramped space by abductors. It was a little larger than a bedroom causing her to feel suffocated. She had been cut off from the rest of the world and stripped of her freedom. Her cell phone had been taken away, leaving her completely isolated from her loved ones. She wasn't even allowed to make a single call. Despite the strict rules, Gail had managed to make a few friends among her colleagues on her work assignment. They too, were forced to work not by choice. However, their conversations were always heavily monitored making it impossible for her to truly connect with them. She longed for a genuine, unfiltered conversation, but that seemed like a distant dream now.

She was paid a wage, oddly enough. But her bank accounts were monitored, and she was constantly reminded that she was under someone else's control. Her salary, which was meant to be a source of freedom and independence, only served as a reminder of her captivity. Gail felt like a puppet, being controlled and manipulated by an unknown force. She couldn't fight back, as much as she wanted to. It was a constant battle between her desire for freedom and her fear of the consequences if she rebelled.

Gail's frustration and hopelessness continued to grow as the days passed. Being high maintenance had always been a part of her identity, but now she found herself letting it slip away. She no longer cared about her appearance; a concept that used to be unthinkable to her. As she looked at her once well-manicured nails, now chipped and partially bitten out of nervousness, she couldn't help but feel a twinge of regret. But she quickly pushed it aside, reminding herself that she had more important things to worry about.

She was only allowed to purchase clothing, toiletry, or pretty much anything from a select list given to her by her abductors. After choosing the things she wanted or needed, they would place the order for her and have them delivered. She used to take great pride in her fashion sense, but now she mostly wore scrubs, the practicality of the uniform far outweighing any desire to look stylish. And when she did have to wear something else, it was usually something cheap and ill-fitting.

Even her hair, something she had always taken great care of, was by far not up to her standards. She had resorted to using a low-grade, drugstore hair dye, unable to afford the salon treatment she was accustomed to. Every time she looked in the mirror, she couldn't help but feel a sense of disappointment and resentment towards her current situation.

Perhaps the biggest blow to Gail's self-esteem was her lack of makeup. She used to never leave the house without a full face that would be perfectly applied, but now she hardly bothered. When she did decide to wear some, it was always a brand that barely lasted a few hours. And as if all of that wasn't enough, Gail's once beloved heels had been replaced with clogs, a practical and comfortable choice, but something she wouldn't be caught dead in out and about. Then there's her once signature scent which was now replaced with a water-based fragrance that went away in minutes, leaving her feeling insecure and self-conscious. Gail knew that these were all small and superficial things in the grand scheme of things, but they were also a constant reminder of the life she had been forced to leave behind.

As Gail sat in her chair gazing out of her window while petting Provolone, she clung to the flicker of hope that burned within her. She dared to dream of a life beyond the confines of her captivity, a life where she could once again walk freely beneath the open sky. But such dreams were tempered by the harsh reality of her circumstances. The specter of death hung heavy in the air, a constant reminder of the perilous tightrope she walked. With Provolone by her side, she vowed to endure, to survive, and to one day reclaim the life that had been stolen from her.

Chapter 4: Dark and Lonely Room

She stood outside the heavy wooden door, his hand trembling as he clutched the key that would grant entry into the lair of secrets that lay beyond. His heart weighed heavy with the burden of the truth he bore, a truth that had shattered the illusion of normalcy and plunged him into a world of darkness and uncertainty.

With a deep breath, he slowly turned the key, the lock clicking open with a finality that echoed through the silence of the house. Stepping inside, he was enveloped by the oppressive stillness of the room, the air thick with the weight of secrets long kept hidden.

As he continued to enter the dimly lit room a heavy silence hung in the air. The only sound was the faint rustle of chains and faint breathing. In the center of the room stood a figure cloaked in shadows, obscured by the darkness that clung over it like a shroud. He slowly approached the dark silhouette searching for any sign of the woman he had once known. But in her place stood a being consumed by the hunger of the night, her eyes gleamed with an otherworldly light that sent shivers down his spine.

Kevin..." Her voice was a haunting whisper, tinged with a hint of the creature she had become. "Please... let me out." But Kevin knew the dangers that lurked beneath her gentle facade. He had seen the beast that lay dormant within her, waiting to be unleashed upon the world. And so, he kept her confined, a prisoner of her own darkness. "I can't, Christine," Kevin murmured, his voice heavy with sorrow. "Not until I find a way to save you."

For a moment it became silent, only the sound of their breath mingling in the stillness of the room. Then, with a suddenness that startled him, Christine briskly jolted forward. Her body bound with chains, she locked a gaze onto his eyes, her eyes burning with a fierce intensity that made him recoil. As he stared back into her eyes, he was yet to understand why Christine, his beloved wife, would now be a creature of the night. Her once gentle features were now twisted by the curse that had befallen her.

Kevin had often seen flashes of the woman she once was, a flicker of humanity amidst the darkness that threatened to engulf her. And in those moments, his resolve faltered, his heart torn between love and duty. But the shadows whispered their warnings, reminding him of the danger that lurked just beneath the surface. And so, he remained steadfast, his love tempered by the harsh reality of their existence.

Almost two years had passed since that fateful vacation, and the shadows that loomed over Kevin's life grew darker with each passing day. The events of that trip had left scars that ran deep, etching their way into the fabric of his very being. Christine bore the brunt of the horrors they had encountered, her once vibrant spirit now hidden behind a dark veil.

In the years since her attack, Kevin had immersed himself in the studies, trying to learn as much as he could about her condition and illness. Desperate to find a cure for the curse that had befallen his wife, the more he had learned the less he understood. Outside the confines of their home, the world continued to turn, oblivious to the silent struggle that raged within their once-loving home. But for Kevin and Christine, each passing day brought them closer to the edge of the abyss, their fate hanging precariously in the balance.

"Dad," a voice called out in the darkness, the sound echoing through the empty attic. Kevin immediately turned around, his heart racing as he saw his son Aaron standing at the entrance. Aaron, now a middle schooler, had just gotten home from school and his presence in the attic was unexpected. "I'll be right there Aaron, go get your homework started," Kevin replied, trying to hide the worry in his voice. But Aaron didn't move, instead slowly leaning over to take a glimpse past Kevin. "But dad, I want to see Chr.." he started to say before Kevin cut him off. "Homework! Now," Kevin yelled out with a stern voice. His frustration and fear bubbled to the surface as he tried to block Aaron's view.

With a heavy heart, Aaron gave his dad a sorrowful look before reluctantly stepping back and closing the door. The weight of the moment hung heavy in the air as Kevin turned back around. But in an instant, his emotions shifted as he realized that Christine was suddenly gone. He quickly took a few steps back in panic as he began to worry that she may have somehow managed to escape.

As fear began to rush over him, he quickened his pace backward, unsure of what to anticipate. Just as he reached the door, he stopped and squinted into the dimly lit attic, spotting a familiar figure. As his vision adjusted, he noticed something glinting on the ceiling. It was Christine, still bound in chains, slowly descending from above hanging upside down with a sly grin on her face, her eyes locked onto Kevin.

"Kevin, let's not be an unkind father. If he wants, he can come to visit me," Christine said, her smirk still present as she gracefully descended from the ceiling, gripping the chains and effortlessly lowering herself. Kevin, realizing Christine was still bound slowly began to walk closer to her, but not too close. "His aroma is one that I find, dare I say, incredibly intriguing. Not like yours, and not like what you have over by the door for me, again," Christine uttered with a cunning tone.

"I will let him come in and see you when you start to feel better, he does miss you," Kevin replied as he walked back towards the door. He then bent down to pick up a book bag, reached inside it, and pulled out a small package. He extended his arm towards the wall near the entrance to the attic, where a series of levers were affixed. With deliberate care, he started to lower one of the levers. This lever was linked to the chains that bound Christine's hands and arm. As the lever was lowered, the chains began to relax, granting her arm a newfound sense of freedom.

Kevin cautiously approached her, gripping his bag tightly. With his bag in hand, he cautiously extended it toward her, maintaining a safe distance while still allowing her to grasp it. Christine's unwavering gaze remained fixed upon Kevin, as she refrained from making any movement towards the bag. For a brief moment, they locked eyes, aching with sorrow and isolation, neither speaking a single word. The weight of their emotions etched on their faces and reflected in their gazes.

As Kevin lifted the bag higher and gradually moved it closer for her to grab, Christine suddenly leaned forward, coming almost nose-to-nose with him. At that moment, her eyes transformed, seemingly radiating a different hue. She then parted her lips, revealing two distinct and pointed canines protruding from the roof of her mouth.

With a swift motion, she snatched the bag from his shaking grip and latched onto one of the chains. She then made her ascent back up the ceiling walls and further back into the dark corners of their home's darkest and loneliest room.

Chapter 5: Caged Secrets

The sound of heavy footsteps echoed down the dimly lit corridor, reverberating off the cold, stone walls of the jail. The cold, metallic bars loomed ominously around Matt as he sat on his narrow bunk, the weight of his secrets pressing heavily on his mind. As he reflected on the questioning he had just endured, he couldn't shake the final words uttered by Sergeant Springer. "Other than your lawyer, the next people you will talk to will expect more answers. My suggestion is that you better spill the beans!"- The words reverberated through his mind.

He couldn't help but wonder if it had all been worth it. The burglary ring, the stolen documents, computers, the accusations, the ominous warnings looming, and the whispered conversations of a world teetering on the brink of chaos. All of it now seemed like a distant bad dream. But amidst the turmoil of his thoughts, one truth remained clear: the threat of Absalom loomed large on the horizon, a harbinger of darkness that threatened to consume them all. Matt had glimpsed the shadows of a conspiracy so vast, so insidious, that even now it frightens him to his core.

With a heavy heart, Matt pondered the consequences of his actions. The government's collusion with the undead, the distribution of tainted vaccines masquerading as salvation. He had stumbled upon a truth that would shake the very foundations of anyone's reality, a truth that could cost him his life.

He then suddenly remembered, in a place known only to his most loyal companion, Matt had meticulously recorded all his discoveries and confidential knowledge, securely preserving them. Each precise record, every classified information, and all of his findings were concealed in the event of an unforeseen occurrence.

The air felt thick with tension, suffocating him with every labored breath as his heart pounded in his chest. He had been thrust into this place only hours earlier, but already it felt like an eternity of dread had settled over him. The secrets he held weighed heavily on his mind, a burden too great to bear in the suffocating confines of his cell. His knowledge was a double-edged sword, granting him power over some and marking him for death by others.

The sound of heavy boots approaching snapped Matt out of his trance, the sudden appearance of two jail officers shattered the silence. As they opened his cell door their imposing figures cast long shadows across the floor. With a cold detachment, they ordered him to stand. With a sinking feeling in the pit of his stomach, he rose to his feet, his hands trembling. They then began ripping through his belongings, searching for any sign of contraband or hidden secrets.

Every inch of his bunk was scrutinized, and every corner of his cell was searched with ruthless efficiency. But despite their efforts, the officers seemed to find nothing of interest, their frustration evident by their exchanged glances. One of them shot Matt a venomous stare, his eyes filled with twisted malice that sent a shiver down his spine. It was a look that chilled him to the core, a stare almost like a glimpse into darkness.

As the two officers left, Matt couldn't shake the feeling of impending doom that hung over him like a dark cloud. Was it paranoia, or had he truly stumbled into a web of deceit far beyond his comprehension? Was he truly alone in this cell, or were there unseen forces lurking in the shadows waiting to strike when he least expected it?

With each passing moment, the world appeared to dissolve into obscurity as he remained motionless in the same spot. His mind was suddenly flooded with a jumble of memories, some from before and some from after the event that had led to his present situation. He found himself overwhelmed with thoughts about the hidden truths that had consumed him, all of which were carefully documented for safekeeping.

And then, figures emerged from the depths of his darkest dreams. His deepest fears merged with reality, blurring the line between nightmare and truth, leaving him unable to discern one from the other. But before Matt could even comprehend what was happening, the world around him began to fade, the edges seemed to drift into nothingness.

Despite the absence of the guards, he was still overwhelmed with dizziness and fear. It was as if the sensation had triggered rapid, oxygen-deprived breaths. His eyes darted towards his rumpled cot, yearning to lay and rest but even then, it felt too far out of reach. The weight of his fear and worry seemed to take a toll on him, resulting in his sight becoming obscured and hazy.

In that final, fleeting moment of consciousness, Matt's gaze fell upon the figures that emerged from the shadows, their presence a chilling reminder of the horrors that lurked in the depths of his mind. Matt couldn't help but wonder if this was truly the end. Had he met his demise at the hands of unseen enemies, or was this merely the beginning of a far darker journey into the unknown? As his vision faded and the world slipped away, the only certainty that remained was the haunting questions that echoed through his mind.

He tried to call out for whatever help he thought he needed but before he could utter a word, the world faded to black, his consciousness slipping away as if swallowed by the abyss. Was he truly alone in the darkness, or was there something far more sinister waiting in the shadows?

Matt's life literally hung there in the balance; his fate entwined with the darkness that began to claim him. His breath shortened as the rope, which seemed to have materialized around his neck in a hazy fog., coiled ever so tightly around his throat. A dark shade engulfed his face as final thoughts echoed in the recesses of his mind. Just as the darkness all but consumed him whole, a solitary figure appeared in the doorway. His expression was unreadable as he looked upon the scene before him. With his one last exhale, Matt's body was still. The guard's countenance and the clinking of the jail cell door were the final sights and sounds that greeted him before the void finally enveloped him.

Chapter 6: A Taste of Fear

Officer Tatum leaned back against the worn leather of the barstool; a grin etched across his face as he surveyed the lively crowd in the dimly lit honkytonk. Tonight, he wasn't Officer Tatum; he was just Travis, out for a night of fun with his buddies, leaving behind the weight of his badge and the memories of his divorce. The air was thick with laughter and the twang of country music, a welcome escape from the routine of his police duties. The dim lights flickered overhead, casting shadows across his face as he clinked glasses with his buddies.

"Another round mother fuckers?" Tatum called out, grinning as he flagged down the bartender. The night was young, and so was he, so at least he felt. He was determined to make the most of his night out and his first night out since his newfound freedom.

As the evening progressed and the whiskey flowed freely, Tatum found himself weaving through the crowded bars of downtown Nashville, his charm and wit on full display. "Hey, Travis, are you to going charm the ladies with those cheesy pickup lines of yours tonight?" one of his friends teased, clapping him on the back. Tatum was a little rusty when it came to flirting seeing it's been a while. But that didn't deter him from dripping the confidence he was known to have.

Tatum chuckled, adjusting his collar with mock arrogance. "Is a pig's pussy pink?" He replied back as to say of course. Laughing, his friends looked at each other and clicked their beers together. Tatum's eyes scanned the room, locking onto a group of ladies sitting at the far end of the bar. With a wink and a slick nod, he made his way over, his confidence still flowing despite his friend's ribbing. The music was blaring, providing the perfect cover for his awkward approach. But Tatum was a charmer, and his game was always on point. Casually dancing to the beat of the music he leaned against the bar and ordered another round of shots. With a sly smile, he delivered his signature pick-up line. "Ladies, I couldn't help but notice you from across the room. You all must be in town for that modeling convention they are having this weekend, am I correct?" The words flowed smoothly from his lips as the ladies giggled. "Oh, nice one there buddy. Probably the best one we've heard all night" one of them replied with a slight grin on her face. Tatum smiled and shrugged his shoulders. "Well, if there were one, you all would definitely be their leading ladies," Tatum quipped with humor and confidence.

As the shots were served, Tatum's buddies joined the party, and the group formed a circle, laughing, joking, and clinking glasses. The night was young, and Travis's newfound freedom tasted sweeter than the whiskey in his glass. He felt alive, his divorce a distant memory, and the weight of his badge long forgotten for now. The country music played on, providing the perfect soundtrack to his night of revelry.

After a while. Tatum and his buddies decided to continue to the next bar, his swagger in full display still. Yet, despite his best efforts, his attempts at wooing the opposite sex seemed to fall flat, each cheesy pickup line met with polite laughter or outright rejection. His friends both egging him on and laughing each time he fell short.

After a few games of pool and darts, Tatum and friends decided they would soon call it a night. As he strolled towards the bar to settle his bill, a wave of joy and contentment washed over him, evoking a newfound sense of rejuvenation. It was as if he had been reborn, a changed man.

As he took a last gulp of the remaining beer that was in his bottle, there in the corner of the bar, he spotted her. She was a vision amidst the swirling noise of the bar, her dark hair cascading over her shoulders like a silken waterfall. Her eyes sparkled with mischief as she caught his gaze, a coy smile playing on her lips. Tatum felt a flutter of nervous excitement in his chest as he watched her, trying hard not to stare. Her beauty and mystery captured his attention like a moth to a flame. With a coy smile, she glanced in his direction, her eyes twinkling with intrigue.

Heart pounding, Tatum downed a shot of liquid courage, not caring that it belonged to someone else who was sitting at the bar beside him. Before sauntering over to her he mumbled some words of encouragement to himself and thought of a perfect approach, his usual confidence waning in the face of her allure. He strode nonchalantly towards her, deliberately adjusting his gait as he approached.

"Hey there, I bet you taste like a bottle of fun, I mean rum," he stated with a smooth and suave demeanor as he stood beside her. Her gaze shifted towards him, a sly grin playing on her lips as she tossed her locks behind her. "Oh, taste huh? That's definitely my favorite sense by far! I just might have to take you up on that offer," she replied as she slowly viewed him up and down with mute satisfaction.

"Is that right? Well, I'm sure my taste buds would just explode if they took just a shot of you! My name is Tatum. What's your name?" He reached out to shake her hand, slowly using his other hand to gently cuff and hold hers. "Well, nice to meet you, Tatum. My name is Cleo." Buoyed by her response, Tatum ordered them both drinks.

Conversation flowed easily between them, punctuated by shared laughter and lingering glances. He began to take note as she declined the drinks he had ordered with a mysterious smile. Shrugging it off, he continued to shoot his best shot at her all while downing the actual shots she had turned down.

Before long, she suggested they continue the conversation at her place, and Tatum eagerly agreed, bidding farewell to his friends with a smug grin. Their impressed gazes followed him as he headed out of the bar with his mysterious companion.

As they climbed into the Uber, Tatum couldn't shake the feeling of anticipation coursing through him, mingled with a hint of apprehension he couldn't quite place. He couldn't help but think in the back of his mind that the situation was far too perfect to be so easy. But he quickly dismissed that thought, telling himself "I guess I still got it after all." The ride to her place passed in a blur of anticipation, Tatum's mind buzzing with thoughts of what awaited him behind closed doors.

As they entered her dimly lit apartment, she disappeared into the shadows, leaving Tatum to explore the cozy living room adorned with vintage records and faded photographs. Slowly, he perused each and every photograph adorning her wall, each giving him a glimpse into her personal life. Pictures of what appeared to be her friends and family lined her walls and counters.

It was then he stumbled upon one particular picture that caught his attention immediately. Its surface and the image of her seemed to be aged, that of a totally different time period altogether. As he continued to study its distant past, a shiver of unease crept down his spine.

Lost in thought, he barely registered her sudden appearance behind him, her figure a tantalizing silhouette against the soft glow of lamplight. His breath caught in his throat as she moved closer, her touch igniting a fire within him that he couldn't deny. There she stood, her presence commanding his full attention.

With a seductive smile, she drew him into her bedroom, her actions swift and purposeful. Tatum's nerves pricked at the back of his mind, but he pushed them aside, surrendering to the intoxicating allure of the moment. As he tried to speak, to voice his concerns, her words cut through the air like a knife. "Stop talking," she whispered, her voice low and hypnotic. Without any warning, she began to take off his shirt and unbuckle his pants, snatching both off and tossing them onto the floor.

Shoving him back against the bed almost effortlessly, she then climbed on top of him. As she straddled him, her movements became more urgent. Grinding back and forth in a way that made sure he could feel the warmth of her in between. Tatum attempted to speak, to question the strange turn of events, but her words silenced him.

And then, in the blink of an eye, everything changed. He watched in shock as fangs descended from her mouth, glinting in the dim light like polished daggers. And in that moment, as realization dawned and fear coursed through his veins, Tatum knew he was in the presence of something far more dangerous than he could have ever imagined.

Chapter 7: Coincidences

Sergeant Springer pushed open the heavy doors of the police department, the morning sunlight filtering through the windows and casting long shadows across the linoleum floor. He was greeted by the familiar bustle of morning activity. With a brisk stride, he made his way through the maze of desks towards his own, a steaming cup of coffee in hand.

But before he could settle into his routine, he detoured towards Detective Moore's desk, curiosity piqued by her diligent focus on the day's tasks. "Morning, Detective," Springer greeted, offering a friendly smile as he leaned against the edge of her desk. "What's on your agenda today?" Detective Moore looked up from her paperwork, a weary smile tugging at the corners of her lips. "Morning, Sergeant. Just diving into a few cold cases that landed on my desk. Got a couple of promising leads on one of them."

Intrigued, Sergeant Springer leaned in closer. "Mind if I take a look?" "Sure, go right ahead." Detective Moore replied without hesitation, handing him the folder. Springer wasted no time flipping through its contents. As he scanned the contents, his eyes narrowed in recognition, a flicker of concern flashing across his features. "Gail Preston," he murmured, his voice tinged with somber recollection. "I remember this one.

Moore nodded; her gaze sympathetic. "Yeah, been missing for almost two years now. Last seen on Christmas morning, sometime right after the downtown bombing." Springer's brow furrowed as memories resurfaced, the pieces of the puzzle slotting into place. "The meeting," he muttered, more to himself than to Moore. "She was with a group of scientists that day." Moore nodded, her expression grave. "That's right. Something about findings on the COVID-19 vaccine. Top secret stuff."

Sergeant Springer nodded solemnly. "Yeah, it's been haunting me since she disappeared. There seem to have been quite a few occurrences and events that have taken place during that particular time that have all appeared to be closely linked to COVID and the vaccine," Springer said still in deep thought. Detective Moore's eyes widened in realization. Silence descended between them as they both absorbed the gravity of the situation. Sergeant Springer shook his head, his expression grave. "I've got a feeling there's more to this case than meets the eye. We need to dig deeper. So yes, please follow up on those new leads and let me know what you all come up with," Springer stated as he glanced at his watch.

As he headed back to his desk, he made sure to stop by the kitchen to top of his cup of coffee. But as he left the kitchen he headed back towards the front of the office, scanning all of the desks on his way. He made his way back to the front of the office where a group of his colleagues stood. "Has anyone seen Officer Tatum?" he inquired, scanning the room once more. The response was unanimous, Tatum was nowhere to be found.

Just then Springer's attention was drawn to the front of the office. Peering out the window, he spotted Officer Greeley disembarking from a vehicle, which appeared to be an Uber. "Why isn't Greeley in his patrol car?" Springer muttered to himself, the puzzle pieces shifting yet again. Confusion furrowed Springer's brow as he approached Greeley, questioning him about the unusual circumstances of his arrival. The laughter of fellow officers echoed in the background as Greeley offered a cryptic explanation, leaving Springer none the wiser. As whispers of Greeley's wreck into a random ditch circulated, Springer couldn't help but shake his head in disbelief. In a department filled with mysteries, both big and small, some things never ceased to amaze him.

Returning to his desk, Springer couldn't shake the feeling that the missing scientist held the key to a puzzle far larger than anyone could have imagined. He once again began to think back to that Christmas morning years ago when he discovered the odd notebook writings. He also began to remember his recent house visit out in Shirley where he recognized the mysterious man who had been in the crowd after the explosion.

As he settled into his seat, he savored a few more sips of his coffee, lost in deep contemplation. Moments later, he started to dismiss it, convincing himself that he was overanalyzing and potentially imagining nonexistent occurrences. Undoubtedly, it was merely a matter of chance, given the fact that it was a tumultuous period for everyone.

As he sat his coffee down on his desk, he reached for his computer keyboard and began to log in at that moment, his gaze lifted and landed on Officer Greeley making his way towards his workstation. A mix of astonishment and dread etched itself across his face. Springer couldn't help but feel that with a look like that on Greeley's face, it was already going to be a long week.

"Sarg, we've got a predicament," Greeley announced, appearing at Springer's desk with a bewildered expression. "What is it," Springer asked. "It's our deranged burglary detainee. He was discovered in his cell last evening, seemingly either a suicide or an attempted suicide." Springer, not understanding what Greeley meant, slowly stood up from his desk. "What? Is it an attempt or is it what it is? I'm confused," he anxiously replied. Due to unknown circumstances, they are maintaining a tight-lipped stance on the matter. Without revealing excessive details, I was essentially informed that this may have been escalated to the FBI at this point."

They both remained quiet for a few seconds trying to understand the reasoning. "Holy Shit," Springer blurted out, finally breaking the silence. "I was literally just contemplating the abundance of bizarre coincidences recently, wondering if I was simply overanalyzing.

However, I have come to realize that that may not be the case," Springer stated as he grabbed his coffee and patrol keys from his desk. "Fuck that, I'm heading down there to see for myself what's going on. Are you going to follow me," he asked Greeley as he began to walk to the door. Springer then came to a sudden halt and turned around. "Oh, that's right! I'll Uber you there," he remarked, making light of Greeley's misfortunate accident.

Chapter 8: Plasmatic

---◆●◆---

The night draped over the city like a velvet cloak, concealing the clandestine activities of its nocturnal denizens. In the heart of the shadows, Sylvester, or Sly, maneuvered a small moving truck through the labyrinthine streets. Rolo, his colleague for the evening's tasks, was seated next to him. Their destination loomed ahead: a small, dilapidated medical clinic that seemed to cower beneath the weight of its own secrets.

The flashing neon sign above the entrance barely spelled out 'Health Clinic,' its letters fading into obscurity. Sly parked the truck at the rear entrance, the building's lights casting eerie shadows across the alleyway. "Alright, Rolo, let's get these crates loaded," Sly said, stepping out of the truck into the cool night air as the moon hung low across the empty back parking lot. Rolo nodded; his crimson eyes gleaming excitedly as they approached the clinic's back entrance door.

Together, they heaved crates labeled "Blood Hub" into the back of the truck, their movements awkward yet determined. Sly stumbled over his own feet more than once, his newfound vampiric agility still eluding him like a prize just out of reach. Rolo, a slightly more seasoned vampire who has mastered the art of blending into the darkness, followed behind with a bemused expression.

As they worked, Sly engaged Rolo in casual conversation, discussing the latest rumors among the vampire community sharing tales of their own struggles with their newfound hunger, and exchanging stories of their misadventures. Sly's antics elicited more than a few chuckles from Rolo, who found amusement in Sly's clumsy nature. Their journey took them to several shadier clinics, each stops a mirror image of the last.

Finally, they arrived at a nondescript warehouse, its steel doors looming like guardians of secrets. Sly and Rolo unloaded the crates, their movements fueled by a sense of urgency mingled with anticipation. Inside the warehouse, Sly's gaze fell upon the rows of crates containing the precious cargo: Alpha Blood. The temptation gnawed at him, urging him to indulge in the somewhat forbidden fruit. But then, a voice echoed in his mind, a warning whispered by Azure, the enigmatic leader of their vampire clan. He remembered her icy gaze, the threat that hung in the air like a promise of doom.

With a heavy heart, Sly tore his gaze away from the tantalizing boxes. He knew the consequences of defying Azure, a risk he couldn't afford to take. As they made their way out of the refrigerated storage, Sly's mind raced with conflicting emotions. The allure of the Alpha Blood tugged at him relentlessly, but he knew that to give in would be to court disaster.

Back at the truck, Sly instructed Rolo to fetch another stack of flyers from the warehouse office. As Rolo read through one of the invitations, Sly couldn't help but marvel at the irony of their situation. What appeared to be a friendly gesture to the unsuspecting public was, in reality, a cunning ploy orchestrated by Azure to further her own agenda. The friendly facade of the community blood drive masked the true purpose behind their actions. To collect as much Alpha Blood as they could.

As Sly and Rolo settled into the seats of the truck after, a sense of accomplishment mingled with anticipation filled the air. Rolo, ever the instigator of mischief, proposed a fitting reward for their night's work: a visit to the notorious bar called "Plasmatic". Sly's eyes lit up with excitement at the suggestion. "Plasmatic it is!" Sly exclaimed, revving up the engine as they sped off into the night. The dim streetlights in this section of the city guided their way to the infamous and low-profile vampire bar.

The entrance of the bar sat hidden, teeming but yet filled with other undead beings. As they stepped inside, the pulsating rhythm of the music enveloped them, a cacophony of beats that seemed to defy categorization. Rolo led the way to the bar counter, exchanging nods and greetings with familiar faces along the way. The bartender, a sly grin playing at the corners of her lips, greeted them with a knowing look.

Rolo leaned into the bartender with a smirk. "What's the special tonight?" The bartender, a sleek and sly figure herself, scanned the menu before listing off a few tantalizing options. "We've got 'O my gosh,' 'AB Fusion,' and for the brave souls, 'Junkies Death.'" Rolo's curiosity was piqued at the mention of the last option. "Junkies Death, huh? What's in that?" The bartender's smirk widened as she explained the drink's ominous name, leaving Rolo chuckling with intrigue. "The name speaks for itself, my friend." He decided to take the plunge and ordered the "Junkies Death" without hesitation.

Meanwhile, Sly couldn't resist asking about a different kind of drink. "Do you have anything with Alpha Blood?" Sly inquired eagerly. The bartender's reaction was less than favorable, her gaze narrowing as she glanced between Sly and Rolo. "Alpha Blood? That's not something we serve here, hon." Realizing his misstep, Sly quickly backtracked and settled for the safer option of an "AB Fusion," his enthusiasm dampened at the implied taboo surrounding his request. The bartender begrudgingly served him, her demeanor frosty as she turned away to attend to other patrons.

As they sat at the bar sipping their drinks and soaking in the atmosphere, a hooded figure caught Sly's attention. Unlike the other patrons, this man stood out like a sore thumb, his humanity apparent to all who crossed his path. Sly's curiosity was in full display, his gaze fixed on the mysterious stranger. He watched intently as the hooded man interacted with the bartender.

A sense of unease settled over him, the man's presence gnawing at his insatiable curiosity.

Rolo followed Sly's line of sight, his own interest sparked by the unusual presence of a human in their midst. They watched as the hooded man approached the bar, engaging in hushed conversation with the bartender. The exchange between the hooded man and the bartender was brief yet cryptic. A sense of intrigue washed over Sly and Rolo as they observed the man was handed what appeared to be a bookbag, and then sliding the bartender something of his own. Their senses were heightened by the air of secrecy surrounding the interaction.

Rolo couldn't resist the urge to inquire further, summoning the bartender over once more. "Who was that guy?" The bartender, her demeanor guarded, revealed his name to be Kevin, a human who had somehow struck a deal with the bar owner to purchase their cocktails. Sly and Rolo exchanged incredulous glances, the implications of a human mingling with vampires in an all-vampire surrounding was rare.

The bartender explained that Kevin's motives revolved around his recently "flipped" wife, a revelation that sent shockwaves through Sly and Rolo's non-existent hearts. Turning a human into a vampire was forbidden without census reporting, a fact that added another layer of intrigue to Kevin's enigmatic presence. As they exchanged glances, a silent agreement passed between them. They would bring this information to Azure, their leader, and uncover the truth behind Kevin's enigmatic presence in their world. After all, in the world of vampires, where secrets and alliances intertwined like threads in a tapestry of darkness, nothing was ever as it seemed. And Kevin's presence in Plasmatic was a mystery begging to be unraveled

Chapter 9: The Upyr Path

In the heart of Nashville, amidst the vibrant streets and bustling commerce, Mayor Terry navigated the delicate balance between public scrutiny and private ambition. Two years had passed since the pandemic, and the city had emerged as a beacon of prosperity under his leadership. Yet, lurking beneath the surface were whispers of scandal and controversy threatening to tarnish his legacy.

Accusations of impropriety followed Mayor Terry, who was no stranger to controversy, like shadows in the night. With his charming demeanor and charismatic presence, he had captured the hearts of many. His reputation as a playboy mayor, entangled in affairs with staff members and even a married city councilwoman whom he had allegedly put on his payroll, cast a pall over his tenure. Allegations of bribery and pay-to-play schemes only fueled the fire, but amidst the turmoil, Nashville flourished.

Amidst the allegations and whispers of scandal, Nashville prospered. Its economy flourished, its population swelled, and jobs abounded. The city gleamed like a jewel in the southern crown, earning its place as the "it" city of America. Mayor Terry remained defiant, buoyed by the undeniable success of its economic resurgence. The city had become a thriving metropolis, attracting droves of newcomers and businesses alike.

On this particular day, Mayor Terry found himself embroiled in the intricacies of city governance, yet his thoughts wandered to the looming specter of re-election. As he exited the parking garage on 3rd Ave, flanked by two of his serious-faced business partners, he couldn't shake the feeling of unease that gnawed at him. It was as if the weight of his secrets bore down upon him.

As they approached the Bell Tech building Mayor Terry's gaze swept over the familiar surroundings. Suddenly, a figure caught his eye lingering in the shadows, a distant observer whose presence elicited a pang of recognition; a silent sentinel watching his every move. But with a heavy sigh, Mayor Terry pushed forward.

Pausing at the entrance, Mayor Terry braced himself for what lay ahead. His footsteps echoed against the pavement as he entered the skyscraper. Inside, the familiar hustle and bustle of city life greeted him as his facade of confidence faltered. He began to conceal the hint of vulnerability he had remaining beneath the surface. As he flirted with a receptionist, his arrogance masked the uncertainty that gnawed at him. As the mayor's demeanor shifted effortlessly, he greeted locals and posed for pictures, his charm masking the turmoil within.

Entering the elevator with practiced ease, one of the gentlemen with Terry initiated a sequence of actions that went unnoticed by all but a select few. Unlocking a hidden compartment at the base of the elevator, the man reached in, pressed a button, and then closed the compartment's door locking it. They then descended into the depths of the building, where secrets lay hidden from prying eyes.

As they entered a dimly lit boardroom Mayor Terry began to check his cell phone, reassured he still could get reception. Suddenly a figure shrouded in mystery and power materialized before them. As the sudden presence stood in the room, the other two men became startled but left him unfazed. Before them stood Talon with an otherworldly presence, a testament to his true nature; an undead, a pureblood. The other two men had their suspicions he could be something otherworldly, but they were still not sure. Being the highest-ranking vampire in his region, Talon held sway over matters that transcended mortal concerns. His presence was a reminder of the delicate balance between the two worlds. His presence was that of one out of the twelve governing forces who make up the Diaeta Assembly: The vampire's highest order.

Talon is well-informed about all that occurs within his domain of North America. He diligently ensures that no vampire transgresses the rules and that the sustenance for his kind remains plentiful. His abode, hidden from human knowledge, remains a mystery. Despite being one of the youngest members of the vampire assembly at 474 years old, he bears the appearance of a 62-year-old human.

In the hushed confines of the boardroom, Mayor Terry and Talon convened, their clandestine meeting shrouded in secrecy. As they discussed matters of utmost importance, the mayor's fate hung in the balance, his future intertwined with forces beyond his control. Mayor Terry expresses gratitude towards Talon for his presence, while Talon nonchalantly dismisses the idea that Terry had a choice in attending.

With expeditiousness, Talon initiated a conversation, probing for intel regarding the current state of "Upath." The term stands for Upyr Path or Pathway. Upath is a groundbreaking communication system that utilizes modern technology and powerful frequencies, enabling the undead to telepathically communicate with one another over greater distances and exert even stronger control over the human mind. Mayor Terry is accompanied by two individuals overseeing the project, yet they are unaware of its complete objectives.

The men explain to Talon the complicities behind the project and why it takes time, but it should be operational in less than a year. The Bell Tech building was selected as the base of operations due to its status as the leading telecommunication and data company in the nation. This expansive facility caters to the entire southern region of the United States, also making it well-equipped to handle vampire communication services.

And then there was one more business matter to be discussed, one of greater importance and secrecy. "Mayor Terry cautiously navigated the conversation as Talon, with a deep baritone, inquired about the enigmatic "Project Princedom Come." The mayor's lack of knowledge was a disadvantage in this clandestine realm, known only to the Diaeta Assembly. Not even the mayor was privy to its purpose, but he was aware of its significance and ties to the very structure they were currently sitting in. Unknown to the mayor what exactly is unfolding there's a secret construction project underway atop the Bell Tech building; directly under where its apexes protrude at its highest points. Talon informs Terry that he plans to ascend to the rooftop to inspect it once the meeting concludes.

As the meeting came to an end, they rose from their chairs, exchanged handshakes, and made their way towards the exit. Suddenly, Talon halted Mayor Terry with a tone that was difficult to decipher. Mayor Terry pivoted to meet Talon's gaze, curious about his intentions. "Your next installment will arrive in the coming days, so stay vigilant," Talon declared with a mixture of satisfaction and evil, slyly winking at him. As his body turned to walk out his thoughts turned as well, grappling with the weight of his decisions.

As they step onto the elevator, one of the men stretches his arm across the door, motioning for Talon to enter. However, Mayor Terry quickly withdraws his hand, stating that Talon doesn't need to use the elevator. As the doors close, the trio share a meaningful and melancholy glance with Talon. For, in the shadows of Nashville's honkytonks and glittering skyline, shadows of power, greed, and corruption danced and fiddled, threatening to consume them all; At least those who still have life.

Chapter 10: Cueball Calathea

The night hung heavy over the city, draped in shadows that danced with the soft glow of moonlight. Amid this nocturnal symphony, Calathea wandered the streets, a solitary figure in the darkness, her senses attuned to the pulse of life around her. Calathea wasn't new to her undead existence, but neither was she old. She was caught in the limbo between innocence and experience, her vampire instincts warring with the remnants of her humanity. She moved with a grace reborn with less than a century of existence, her amber eyes scanning the urban landscape with a mixture of caution and curiosity. As she moved silently through the night, a voice cut through the darkness, sharp and commanding. "Hey, you there!"

Calathea froze, her muscles tensing as she turned to face the source of the voice. Standing before her was Azure, a figure bathed in moonlight, her presence both alluring and intimidating. Calathea hesitated, unsure of what to do. Azure, ever watchful, sensed her presence long before she came into view. The scent of vampires lingered in the air, a tantalizing fragrance that stirred memories of ages past. With a knowing smile, Azure called out to the mysterious young one, her voice a melodic whisper in the night. "Come on, don't be shy," Azure said with a smirk, gesturing for Calathea to approach. "I won't bite... unless you want me to of course."

Despite her apprehension, Calathea found herself drawn to Azure's confidence. She cautiously made her way towards the other vampire, her eyes never leaving Azure's piercing gaze. "Calathea," Azure purred, her tone laced with intrigue. "Come closer, dear. There's no need to be shy." Calathea hesitated, uncertainty flickering in her gaze like a fleeting shadow. But something in Azure's demeanor, a blend of confidence, allure, and the fact that she somehow knew her name beckoned her forward. With cautious steps, she approached the sleek black car Azure leaned against, a glimmer of curiosity lighting her eyes.

Once Calathea was within reach, Azure motioned towards her car. "Get in. We need to talk." Calathea hesitated before relenting, sliding into the passenger seat beside Azure. As she settled into the passenger seat beside Azure, the air crackled with unspoken tension. Azure's eyes gleamed with a mixture of amusement and appraisal, her lips curling into a sly smile as she studied her newfound companion. "Is it safe to assume that you are aware of what I am?" Inquired Azure. "Of fucking course, there exists a possibility that you would have been devoured before you could even enter the car. However, my awareness of your true nature does not necessarily ensure your safety as I may not be inclined to consume you, but that does not diminish the danger you pose.

Azure, rich with amusement replied, "You're a bold one, aren't you? Wandering the streets alone, without a care in the world. Tell me, Calathea, what brings you to these dark corners of the city?" Calathea shifted uneasily, her gaze flickering away from Azure's penetrating stare. "I... I was just... exploring," she murmured, her voice tinged with uncertainty. Azure chuckled softly, a sound like velvet wrapped in steel. "Exploring, you say? My dear, you're not like the others. There's a fire in your eyes, a hunger that sets you apart. I can see it, even in the dimmest of lights. Let's go for a ride young one." Calathea appeared indifferent and unbothered, simply sitting still while turning her head to gaze out of her passenger side window.

As they drove through the labyrinthine streets, Azure's curiosity continued to simmer beneath the surface like a coiled serpent. She prodded and probed, unraveling the threads of Calathea's past with a delicate touch that belied her true intentions. "So, tell me, Calathea," Azure began, her voice a soft whisper in the stillness of the car. "Where do you stay? How have you managed to evade the eyes of your kind for so long, without the guidance of an older vampire to watch over you?" "How can one determine whether I have received any quote-unquote guidance or not," Calathea retorted in a condescending tone. With a sly expression, Azure glanced at Calathea and confidently declared, "I don't make determinations. I am certain!"

Calathea's heart skipped a beat at Azure's words, a mixture of fear and exhilaration coursing through her veins. She had never encountered anyone like Azure before, someone who saw beyond the surface to the darkness that lurked within. "So, what's your story?" Azure asked, her tone laced with genuine interest.

Calathea hesitated, unsure of how much to reveal. gaze darkened with a shadow of sorrow, her past a tapestry of pain and loneliness. But there was something about Azure that put her at ease, something that made her want to open up. So, she began to speak, her words spilling out in a rush. Azure listened intently; her expression unreadable. After Calathea was done speaking, Azure inquired., "And how have you managed to stay under the radar for so long? No coven?" Calathea shrugged, a smile tugging at her lips. "Luck, I guess. And a healthy dose of paranoia." Azure chuckled, the sound low and melodious. "Well, luck has brought you to me, my dear. And I have big plans for you." Calathea's curiosity piqued. "Plans?"

With a smirk still plastered on her face, Azure proceeded to pull off the road and into a nearby parking lot. Calathea, just then noticing they were at what seemed to be a bar or a pub, leaned over to look out the window to read the sign. "Plasmatic? I've heard of this place." As Azure exited the vehicle, she swung the door open and stepped gracefully onto the pavement. Taking a moment to glance back at Calathea, she leaned her head back into the car. "Well, now you will be doing more than just hearing about the place. Come in with me really quick, I have to talk to someone for a second."

Upon entering the bar, they both halted in their tracks as Azure surveyed the crowd with a vamp-like intensity. At that moment, her eyes locked onto the figure she had been seeking: Sly, who was in the middle of a game of pool and preparing to make his move. As he prepared to strike with his cue, the balls scattered in every direction, effortlessly rolling into a pocket as if guided by an invisible force.

Sly bolted upright and hung his head low as if he were fully aware of the situation. The remaining figures at the table rose with a mixture of bewilderment and fury. "That's bullshit motherfucker, you either just cheated or someone helped you, either way, you're going to pay the fuck up! You know the goddamn rules!" Just then Sly, still looking straight ahead yelled out," Thanks a fucking lot Azure!" Azure and Calathea made their way to the table where the others had been engrossed in their game. As they proceeded, their way began to part, making a path, allowing them to pass through as everyone stepped to the side. As they reached the table, Sly turned to face them. The rest of the undead nearby glanced at Azure, then quickly retreated to their seats, their expressions a blend of trepidation and reverence.

"Hello Sly," Azure exclaimed, flashing a mischievous yet playful smile. Sly pivoted, casting a disconsolate expression towards Azure before shifting his gaze to Calathea. "You messed up my game, thanks. And who the hell is that?" Sly and Calathea engaged in a fierce stare-down, their eyes locked in a challenging gaze, as though they were sizing each other up. "That is my soon-to-be self-appointed mini-me. But currently, that is not something you need to worry about. You indicated you have something to inform me about, so step into my office."

Azure turned to Calathea, "I need to have a quick talk with Sly here, if you'd like you can wait at the bar, and order anything, I'll make sure it's on the house." Calathea, who didn't seem to hear a word Azure was saying, had her eyes focused on the pool table. She then turned and looked at Azure, "Thank you, I'm good, I'll be right here." She then quickly turned around and yelled out to everyone near the billiard table. "Since Sly got shit to do at the moment, I'm the mother fucking replacement! So, one of you get your little bitch ass up, and let's play!" With a proud smile from ear to ear, Azure turned and faced Sly, "I've found my cue ball! Come on."

Chapter 11: Before The One, Comes One

In the heart of the Gideon mountains, shrouded in secrecy and shadow, the Diaeta Assembly convened in their secret chamber. Twelve powerful pureblood vampires, each bearing the weight of their territories, gathered around the marble round table, their presence a sinister specter in the dimly lit chamber. Before the meeting could commence, a solemn hush fell over the assembly as they rose for a quick prayer to honor Absalom, the Vampire God, the forgotten son of King David. Their voices, low and reverent, filled the chamber with an eerie resonance, invoking the ancient deity's name.

"In the shadows deep, where darkness reigns,

We gather here, in silent refrains.

To Absalom, the king's forgotten son,

Whose legend lives, his will be done.

Gatekeeper to immortality's door,

We come before you, our hearts implore.

> We gather now, prepared for thy return,
>
> With thy army vast, our foes to spurn.
>
> For when thou cometh, with darkened might,
>
> We will revel in the eternal night.
>
> All of mankind will be no more than prey,
>
> Only for our pleasure, they'll wither away.
>
> Oh, dear leader, hear our fervent plea,
>
> Continue to guide us, our souls set free.
>
> In thy name, we all stand tall,
>
> And until the day darkness claims all.
>
> Absalom Absalom Absalom Absalom!

With their prayer complete, the Diaeta 12 settled back into their seats, their hooded cloaks concealing their features in the dim light. It was time for the roll call, a ritualistic introduction that reaffirmed their identities within the assembly. "Let us announce ourselves before our lord Absalom," Seneca announced, her voice commanding attention. One by one, the assembly stood to speak their names, their voices echoing through the chamber like whispers of the night. Dion. Seneca.

Calliope. Amis. Cassia. Athalia. Kushim. Pazia. Galla. Vita. Carolus. and finally, Talon.

With the introductions complete, the assembly began to delve into discussions about their respective territories and taxes. Seneca meticulously examines the financial contributions of their district, armed with a notebook resembling that of a scribe, to ensure that they are all aligned and following expectations. This was a testament to the assembly's control over their domains. After completing her audit, she gazes up and gives a satisfied nod.

The next order of business; Alpha Blood. This blood was the potent elixir that promised strength and power to those who drank it. The blood, harvested from the younger alpha generation vaccinated with the COVID-19 vaccine, held the promise of strength and power. A group of covert scientists collaborated with the Diaeta to incorporate an additional element into the vaccine, guaranteeing its infusion into the bloodstreams of individuals, specifically the youth. This final addition served as the ultimate cocktail component, the ideal mixture for a superstrength vampire vigor. This precious blood type is to be the key to Absalom's prophesied return, a prophecy that loomed large over the assembly's ambitions.

Talon, responsible for overseeing the bulk of the alpha blood supply held by Azure, assured the assembly that it was safe and secure. However, suspicions lingered among some members, wary of Azure's ambitions and resentments. Talon's territory came under scrutiny. Some members harbored suspicions of Azure's intentions, believing her to be power-hungry and resentful of her overlooked status in the Diaeta hierarchy of North America.

As they discussed a solution to ease their worries, the assembly voted to summon Azure to their chambers for interrogation in the very near future. Talon agreed to deliver the message upon his return, pledging to ensure Azure's compliance and allegiance.

The final matter at hand was "Project Princedom Come." This undertaking included a superior technological device constructed atop the "Bell Tech" building in Nashville, Tennessee. This device is believed to open a portal for Absalom's return and the arrival of his army. This project, also overseen by Talon, further solidified his influence within the assembly. Talon has once again affirmed that its project is progressing as intended and has taken great care to ensure that all participants are putting forth their utmost efforts to bring it to fruition.

After the meeting's conclusion, a fellow member revealed an unexpected delight for those in attendance - a lavish feed to satisfy their innermost cravings and offer a reverent tribute to their deity, Absalom. Just then, three ominous boxes slowly descended from the ceiling, their contents hidden from view. Servants emerged, bearing chalices for each member, as anticipation hung heavy in the air. With a clap of his hands, The server in charge of the special feeding motioned for the contents of the crates to be unveiled.

Suddenly, metallic-like sounds echoed from within the boxes, followed by the desperate cries and screams of trapped human beings. As the cries of suffering and torment grew in intensity, crimson liquid started to trickle from protrusions on every enigmatic container. As the blood poured out, the assembly watched in morbid fascination. Each member was instructed to pour themselves a cup of the rarest, freshest blood - harvested from humans, fed to die for this very purpose. One by one they all filled their cups to the brim, enjoying their macabre feast.

With each sip, they savored the taste of their victims' final moments, their thirst for power and dominance unquenchable in the darkness of the night. It is a paradoxical situation where the very laws imposed upon their subjects are the very same laws that they themselves choose not to follow. They believe they are exempt from these laws, handpicked by the almighty Absalom. There is no doubt that the assembly's hypocritical behavior has very well caught the attention of specific individuals within the undead population. But for now, as the screams faded into silence and the blood flowed freely, the Diaeta Assembly reveled in the moment.

As the last drops of blood were savored and the echoes of their twisted feast faded into the darkness, their senses heightened, and a sudden chill swept through the

Diaeta Assembly chamber. A mysterious figure, materialized before them, slipping through the chamber doors like a thief in the night shrouded in a cloak of darkness. Instantly, the assembly erupted in outrage and alarm. Anger simmered beneath the surface as they demanded to know who dared to intrude upon their sacred gathering.

Rising to their feet with primal fury, they began to unleash their vampiric powers, only to be repelled by an unseen force emanating from the hooded figure. But their attempts to confront the figure were met with a force beyond their comprehension, as unseen energy sent them crashing back to the floor. Forced back to their seats stunned and bewildered, they watched in trepidation as the figure approached the table, his presence an enigma glowing from his entire body. With a flourish, the figure pulled back the hood of his cloak, revealing a face shrouded in radiant light, features obscured yet mesmerizing.

In a voice that echoed with otherworldly power, the figure spoke. "Absalom has heard your prayers," the figure proclaimed, his voice resonating with divine authority. "The time is nigh for his return, but before him shall come his son, a harbinger of darkness who shall pave the way for Absalom's imminent return and supreme reign." The assembly listened in stunned silence as the figure revealed the identity of Absalom's son. Shock rippled through the air at the revelation, their minds reeling with the implications of this unforeseen twist.

The son would be none other than Vladislaus Dracul, known by many names throughout history, including The Impaler and The Count. His name hung heavy in the air, a precursor of doom and destruction for mankind. Gasps of disbelief echoed through the chamber as the Diaeta 12 grappled with the revelation. With a solemn warning to prepare for the coming storm and before they could fully comprehend the magnitude of the revelation, the temple itself seemed to tremble and quake with a deafening roar. The chamber doors burst open, unleashing a wave of primal energy that felt as if it had shaken the stone foundation to its core.

As they shielded their eyes from the blinding light, the mysterious figure vanished into the shadows, leaving the assembly in a state of bewilderment and awe. And as the doors slammed shut once more, the chamber fell into an eerie silence leaving them all with both excitement and a tinge of fear of what was to come.

Chapter 12: "Excuse Me, Did You Say Something?"

---—◆•●•◆—---

cool gust of wind swept through the air, carrying with it the sweet symphonies of chirping birds. The sun's vibrant rays stretched out as if eagerly welcoming the new day. The setting was serene, with the gentle rustling of leaves and the distant sounds of nature filling the atmosphere. The clouds seemed to glide through the sky, mimicking the gentle undulation of the ocean's waves. The soft caress of the breeze flowing through the canopy's fabric created a whimsical yet comforting sensation, akin to a gentle and calming tickle. As his gaze slowly came into focus, he couldn't help but ponder that, had he not known any better he may have mistaken his surroundings for paradise or even heaven.

In an instant, it dawned on him that the formations in the sky were not clouds, but rather a design on the ceiling. And he was not in a heavenly or idyllic place. "You Fucking Bitch!" he roared, jolting up and swiftly tumbling off the bed and onto the floor!

In a swift motion, he extended his arm over the bed and used it to hoist himself up, still staying partially hidden from view. The top of his head poked out from the side of the bed. His eyes shifted back and forth looking for any sign of whoever or whatever it was that he was with the night before.

Glancing to the side, he spotted his pants and shirt, neatly folded on the nightstand next to the side of the bed where he had been sleeping. As he hastily snatched up his clothes, he detected a foreign scent of laundry detergent and fabric softener, as though they had been washed and dried. Instead of standing up, he quickly put on his clothes while still lying on the floor hopefully not being seen. He then thought to himself, now if only I could find my socks and shoes.

On a mission to leave undetected as soon as possible, he then crawled around to the front of the bed. He suddenly came to a halt upon hearing a voice. He looked around to see where it was coming from, and that's when he noticed the bathroom door was halfway ajar. He wondered if that was where his shoes were, so Tatum slowly crawled in that direction. As he reached the door, still down on his knees, he stopped dead in his tracks. It was the voice again. It was a woman singing and the sound of water dripping. "Fuck, Fuck, Fuck," he whispered as he came to the sudden realization that the woman he longed to distance himself from was immersed in the bathtub.

Slowly back crawling away from the door, he quickly slid to the side of the bed once again, afraid to go past the bathroom and possibly risk being seen. Pausing to figure out his next move, he started to think to himself.

"Wait, this is fucking weird. What in the hell happened? If I was in danger, why am I still here and she's just relaxing in the bathtub as if nothing happened? Or did something happen?"

"Nothing happened silly," a voice suddenly replied, startling Tatum to the point he almost yelled. He then quickly stood up and began to walk backward almost into the wall. There she was standing in front of him with a grin. She stood draped in a towel from her breast down, another towel wrapped around her hair and gently cleaning her ears with a Q-tip. "How the fuck did you know what I was thinking, lady?" Tatum inquired, still shaken by her sudden presence.

"Let's see, you're crawling on the floor hiding as if you are trying to hurry up and get the fuck out of dodge. Of course, I know what you are thinking, man," she quipped. "No, you don't know what I'm thinking. What I'm thinking is that you tried to attack me with those... those..those... things lady or whatever the entire fuck you are!" With a look of confusion and slight amusement, she took a break from cleaning her ears and walked closer to Tatum. "In case you forgot, my name is Cleo. And what "things" was I trying to attack you with? These?" Cleo then slowly pulled down her towel showing him her breast.

After a brief pause, Tatum took a moment to survey what was in front of him before quickly regaining his composure. "No! Don't you try that again! That's what you tried to pull last night before you attacked me. Well, almost, or what the fuck ever you did," he declared with utmost gravity. Seeing that Tatum was serious she pulled her towel back up and stepped back, giving him space. "Sweetie, first of all, I never did such a thing. You were pretty hammered and ended up falling asleep as soon as I fixed myself on top of you. Secondly, that wasn't last night honey, that was the night before. You've been passed out since then for the most part. I had nothing on my schedule yesterday, so I just let you sleep it off. I actually enjoyed watching you sleep and having you here. Well, that is until now!"

Tatum stood silent for a few moments trying to process what Cleo had just said. "Did you just say it's NOT yesterday, today is actually the next day after that?" he asked, befuddling his words in a slight panic. "Isn't it always? But yes, it is," she replied with a hint of sarcasm. "Oh great, I'm supposed to be at work by now," Tatum stated as he began to look around the room. "Have you seen my shoes and my phone?" Before he could finish asking, she had already left the room to retrieve them.

As he walked out of the room, he met her in the hallway with his items. They slowly made their way to her living room where he plopped down on the couch to put on his socks and shoes and then to scroll through his phone. "If you need a ride back to your car Travis, I don't mind taking you. That's if you're not afraid I will attack you," Cleo said with an unsure grin. Looking up from his phone he let out a guilty sigh. "Look, I'm sorry. I guess I was pretty trashed. It seemed so real though, but maybe it was just all the things going through my head at the time. But thank you, I have an Uber coming. I need to clear my head and think of something to tell my boss by the time I reach the house. But, if you're free later this week, I wouldn't mind trying it again. Well, minus all the shots and comatose." They both began to laugh as she reached for his phone to put her number in it. As she handed him the phone back, she made sure he could see the name she saved it under. "Lady," Tatum said as he chuckled even harder.

As Tatum sat in the back seat of the Uber, he quietly stared out the window still trying to piece together everything that happened. He felt embarrassed a little but from what he could tell she didn't seem to mind. He then remembered the pictures on her wall that appeared to be from a whole different time period. If those pictures were those old-timer photos they take at carnivals and fairs, the photographer must've done a really good job. He also remembered that as he was looking through some of her other mementos, he came across her full first and last name. "Cleopatra Laney," Tatum said to himself. Being a police officer has its perks, so he'll be doing some quick research of his own. "Excuse me, sir? Did you say something?" The Uber driver asked Tatum as he peered through his rearview mirror. "No sir. Just talking to myself!"

Peering out the window, Tatum began to think what he would tell Springer. He wasn't worried about getting in any trouble really, but he would rather he not know he was hammered and imagined his date to be a gorgeous vampire who put a spell on him causing him to sleep for two days. He couldn't help but think how ridiculous that sounded and how drunk he must've been to think such a thing was real. As he laughed under his breath still gazing out the window, he looked over at the car next to him. It was another Uber driver.

Tatum and the Uber driver exchanged a quick smile. He then glanced at the passenger in the back seat who didn't seem to notice Tatum. He then leaned up and squinted his eyes to get a better look at the passenger. "No way! What the hell is this shitbrain doing in an Uber when he's supposed to be out patrolling?" Tatum asked himself under his breath. It was Officer Greeley in the back seat of the other Uber. That's when Tatum decided he had better lean down in the seat so as not to be seen. "I sure have been doing a lot of ducking and hiding today and it's not even noon yet," Tatum uttered to himself. The Uber driver peered in his review mirror once more, "Excuse me, sir, did you say something?"

Chapter 13: Whispers of Rebellion

The fluorescent lights hummed overhead as Gail sat in her cramped workstation, surrounded by vials, pipettes, and microscopes. The facility's walls still seemed to close in as she continued to meticulously follow the instructions laid out before her. She toiled under the watchful eyes of her captors, her every move monitored, her every action dictated by unseen hands. But on this particular day, as she diligently followed the orders given to her, a glimmer of opportunity presented itself.

Almost as if destiny had a hand in the matter, a file had been carelessly left accessible on the computer of the chief overseer, whose office was mere steps away. She cautiously avoided drawing attention to herself as she quickly scanned the area, attempting to decipher the subject of the file from where she was seated. If any time was a perfect time to make her move, it was then.

Gail initially hesitated, her heartbeat accelerating with the fear of being caught. However, she soon remembered that the head supervisor, who had been accessing the files on his computer, had just finished indulging in a huge lunch consisting of three massive burritos. She was well aware that after every Mexican feast, the chief would grab a publication from his desk and retreat to the restroom for half an hour, and today was no exception. Also, during that time of day, no one else would normally be on the floor in that area as they would be down at lunch.

Driven by her intense curiosity, she couldn't resist the urge to sneak a glimpse, perhaps even explore further with a few clicks. She nonchalantly rose from her chair and stealthily entered his office without being noticed. With great speed, she started clicking through the documents, swiftly scanning them with her gaze. At that moment, she realized the significance of the files, as the words "top secret" were highlighted in crimson at the base of the file heading.

Despite the sensitive document warning, she proceeded and stumbled upon a discreet file labeled "Project Alpha Gen." This sparked her curiosity and she delved into the contents of the file. What she discovered sent shivers down her spine, as she came across her own name boldly mentioned on the 4th page of the document. Despite her desire to read as much as she could right then and there, she realized that wouldn't be unwise. The sheer volume of over 10,000 pages was overwhelming and she knew her time was limited and would be unsure where to begin. She then remembered she had a small USB storage disc in her pocket she had used earlier which had ample space.

With trembling hands, she plugged in the USB storage chip, her pulse racing as she initiated the download. Anxiety clawed at her, each passing second feeling like an eternity. She paced the room, stealing nervous glances at the door, her mind consumed by the fear of being caught.

As she skimmed through a few pages while it was downloading, the magnitude of what she was reading stole her breath. A glimpse into the truth she had been denied for so long unfolded before her, a web of deceit and manipulation woven by unseen forces. She had unwittingly become a pawn in a game far larger than she could have ever imagined. Each passing second felt like an eternity as she frantically waited for the file to be completed, her senses on high alert for any sign of being caught.

As the download bar slowly ticked closer to completion, she meticulously tallied the remaining percentage as if it were a countdown from 10 to 0. Just as the final seconds ticked away, she succeeded, withdrawing the chip from the computer just in time to evade detection. With a racing heart, she left the office and returned to her workstation no more than five seconds before the head overseer came through the hallway door and to his office. The weight of her newfound knowledge was heavy upon her shoulders.

Later that afternoon, back in the confines of her small apartment, Gail poured over the contents of the file, her emotions a tumultuous whirlwind of disbelief, anger, and sorrow. The truth laid bare before her was more horrifying than she could have ever imagined—the manipulation of vaccines, the exploitation of innocent lives, and the existence of vampires lurking in the shadows. As she read, tears stung her eyes, her heart heavy with the weight of the knowledge she now possessed. She was confronted with the extent of the deception, the lives unwittingly placed in jeopardy by the machinations of those in power.

Rest eluded her that night as her mind churned with possibilities. She yearned to expose the truth, to break free from the chains that bound her to this place of darkness and deceit. But amidst the despair, a spark of determination ignited within her. She couldn't undo the past, but she could do her best to expose the truth and make them pay for what they had done; not just to her but to everyone, especially the younger generation. As she reflected on that Christmas morning meeting many years ago, she couldn't help but ponder how close she had been to the discovery. Instead of wallowing in self-pity for being uprooted from her familiar life, she now believed it had happened for a purpose. She felt destined to be where she was, to bear witness, and illuminate the truth behind the events that were currently unfolding.

In the days that followed, Gail meticulously planned her next move. She studied the overseers' routines, mapping out their movements with precision. She needed to get this information out as soon as possible. And when that moment arrived, she would need to move with precision and send the damning files to someone she trusted and who could help her bring the truth to light.

Due to the blocking of all communication with the outside world, she and the others who were here against their will were also unable to send any form of correspondence. This included sending emails unless it was to those within the facility. The only individuals with access to devices that could transmit data were the higher-ranking officials and the overseers, such as the computer she had received the file in question.

Finally, after about a week, she felt she was ready to make her move. Sending the files out would indeed take longer than it did downloading them. But she felt she had a plan that would work as that moment had finally arrived. She also knew who she would be sending the information out to. It would not only be someone who would believe it, but would get the word out, and possibly track down the IP address leading them to her location.

With precision, she acted and waited for the opportune moment to strike. Through sly manipulation, she convinced the overseer to order from a specific restaurant, not by telling him, but by discussing it in his presence, with someone else. She carefully described the cuisine, exaggerating its excellence. Unbeknownst to him, the food was known to cause quick and frequent bathroom trips. This allowed her ample time to access his computer and send the files out. She hoped that he would be so consumed by his urgent need to use the bathroom that he would forget to lock his computer. And, as she had anticipated, her clever plan was successful.

As the files were transferred and she quickly exited the overseer's office undetected, a sense of relief washed over her, followed by an unexpected surge of joy. She couldn't contain her smile nor suppress the elation bubbling inside her throughout the day. It was a risky move, but it was the right one, and for the first time in years, she allowed herself to feel hope. She not only felt it, but she also wore it on her face.

Unbeknownst to Gail, her sudden shift to a more upbeat behavior had not escaped the notice of her peers and overseers. While she may have thought she had successfully executed her scheme, another watchful supervisor had taken note of her peculiar change in mood sensed the stirring of something sinister and felt a whisper of rebellion in the air.

Chapter 14: A Series of Recurring Coincidences

---◆●◆---

Sergeant Springer's arrival at the home was met with a scene of controlled chaos. Marked and unmarked vehicles lined the street, agents scurried about ferrying boxes and evidence from the premises. Sergeant Springer parked his car along the crowded South Nashville road. He stepped out of his patrol vehicle, the air thick with tension as agents bustled about, boots crunched against the gravel.

Among the familiar faces, he spotted Agent Gibbs, a longtime friend and former colleague. They exchanged nods, their camaraderie forged in the crucible of past investigations, now reunited on the threshold of a new mystery. They had weathered storms together and faced down threats, but nothing quite like the enigma they now found themselves entangled in. Agent Gibbs, a former Sergeant in the police force, had recently made the transition to becoming an FBI agent. This occurred at a similar time when Springer was promoted to the rank of Sergeant following his tenure as a detective.

Gibbs walked over and greeted Springer with a handshake while giving him a proud look. "Now that uniform looks good on you brother. I know you've been a Sarge for a while but still, congratulations," Gibbs stated as he patted Springer on the back." "Thanks, and the new agent look isn't so bad either," Springer replied. "Well, it pays the bills, and it keeps me knee-deep in shitshows such as this one," said Gibbs as he motioned for Springer to come with him inside.

The house they had raided belonged to, none other than, Matt Potts. The name had surfaced in connection with the recent string of burglaries during recent months in the downtown area. But what had begun as a routine investigation had morphed into a full-blown web of conspiracies. As Gibbs led him into the house, Springer's senses were assailed by the condition it had been kept in. Descending into the basement, Springer's gaze swept over the scattered remnants of Potts' illicit activities which appeared to be files and computers stolen from businesses across the city.

"The pieces don't quite fit together," Gibbs commented, a hint of exasperation in his tone. "There are recorded payments to unfamiliar parties, dealings with no traceable records, transactions made through shelf corps. Of course, this all belongs to the business owners since it's stolen property. What truly confounds me is the reason behind the theft of these items. It appears that a significant portion of the goods that were stolen from the businesses consist of items that were being held on behalf of other businesses and organizations. "Springer nodded, his mind racing with possibilities. "It was as if the businesses targeted by Potts and his cohorts were unwittingly or wittingly harboring secrets of far darker purposes.," replied Springer. "And of course, it sucks ass that he had to off himself last night. The little twerp might have been on to something," Potts stated with frustration.

Among the chaos, Springer's attention was drawn to a particular set of documents and files, Print Pros Plus, one of the businesses targeted by Potts and his cohorts. Memories of their encounter with Potts flashed through Springer's mind, intertwined with the grim fate of the business owner who had also taken his own life in the wake of the burglary.

As he continued to sift through the Pro Prints Plus documents, Springer's fingers alighted upon a set of what appeared to be schematics. The blueprint was for some unknown machine, alongside detailed floor plans of the "Bell Tech" building. It all was just more added pieces to the puzzle falling into place but still with clarity. "Why does there always seem to be a connection to the Bell Tech Building?" Springer murmured; his voice heavy with unease. "That's where the bodies are buried," Gibbs' response was cryptic, tinged with the weight of centuries-old whispers of rituals, sacrifices, and other dark secrets that had taken place on that same land.

Having inspected a few of the stolen belongings in the basement, Springer sought permission to briefly view Matt's bedroom also. With Gibbs in concurrence, they made their way there. As they entered Matt's room, they noticed the walls were adorned with bizarre writings and drawings reminiscent of another encounter in the past, Allen the suicide bomber, his memory still haunting the edges of their consciousness. As Springer quickly read over some of Matt's writings, it all reminded him of Matt's interrogation recently and some of the things he had said during.

Springer then stopped at a note that was tacked to the wall that appeared to be a poem. Grabbing Gibb's attention, he began to read the writing out loud.

"I seek out what may, I seek out what might.
I seek out for certain a meal for tonight.
One who lay down their head for the night.
One who, for certain, won't see the sunlight.
Right now, they may pray, but before morning they'll cry.
For the blood of an Alpha will rain from the sky.
So, child, close your eyes and dream happy dreams.
Those of pretty butterflies, mountains, and streams.
Fantasies of chocolates, candies, and ice cream.
For in the morning, Mommy and Daddy will awaken to screams.
Those dreams will become nightmares from the terror above.
Then, fall to those valleys and streams with a thud.
So be sure in your dreams to give them all of your love.
For the sun brings new life, and so will your Alpha Blood!"

With a look of confusion, they both glanced at each other for a few seconds and headed out the door.

Upon stepping outside, Springer's gaze fixated on strange inscriptions adorning the door frames and windows. He turned to Gibbs and inquired about their purpose. Gibbs, remembering Allen had mentioned something similar in his writings before, explained that it was an ancient script that wards off malevolent spirits. The writings were said to prevent any unwelcome entities from entering, even if they were invited. With the markings by the entrances, the creatures could not enter nor penetrate, no matter the circumstance. Springer, still perplexed, exited the front door.

Together, they stepped out into the fading sunlight, the weight of their discoveries hanging heavy in the air. But as they parted ways, a nagging feeling lingered. They found themselves questioning their roles in law enforcement causing them to be solely fixated on tangible evidence, rather than giving adequate attention to inexplicable occurrences that warranted further scrutiny.

In recent years there's been a plethora of coincidental events that have taken place. This leads to the need for further investigation into the underlying causes of these numerous coincidences. Then there's always a chance that these occurrences are not mere coincidences but are significant events occurring in our midst. We perceive them as coincidences because certain crucial pieces of the entire picture are being deliberately concealed.

Chapter 15: Azure's SLY Plan

The night air wrapped around Azure and Sly like a blanket as they stepped out of the dimly lit vampire bar, *Plasmatic*. The neon lights from the establishment flickered behind them as they moved away from the entrance, seeking the quiet solitude of a secluded corner. Azure's mind buzzed with determination, her thoughts swirling like the shadows dancing on the pavement.

"Alright, Sly," Azure began as they found a spot away from prying ears, "I know you've got something to inform me of, but first, I need to know if I have your full support." Sly's expression was unreadable in the darkness, but his voice held steadfast resolve. "You know you do, Azure. Anything you need, I'm there." His response was swift and resolute, his loyalty unwavering in the face of Azure's steely gaze.

Azure's lips curled into a dangerous smile at Sly's words, her eyes flashing with a predatory gleam. "Good," she purred, her voice low and hypnotic. "Because we're going to need all the help we can get. and I'm done playing by the rules," she declared. I'm tired of dancing around the Diaeta Assembly, pretending to respect their God awful, or should I say Absalom awful, archaic ways."

As they spoke, the darkness seemed to thicken all around them. Azure's mind raced with possibilities, her thoughts a whirlwind of strategy and calculation. She knew the risks of challenging the Diaeta Assembly and defying their authority, but she also knew that the rewards far outweighed the risks. With a fierce intensity, Azure laid bare her plans for rebellion, her desire to either take a seat at the table forcefully or simply take full control of the Diaeta Assembly, even eliminating them if needed.

"Talon will be our first target." Her voice cold and calculating. "Once he's out of the damn way, the rest of the Assembly will fall like dominoes." Sly nodded in agreement, his eyes fixed on hers as she spoke. Talon, the governor of their territory was a symbol of everything she despised about the entrenched hierarchy. "They think they can control us with their empty promises and ancient prophecies," Azure spat, her frustration boiling to the surface.

Her grip tightened on Sly's arm, her eyes blazing with determination. "I'm just as old, just as powerful as any of them. The Diaeta Assembly, with its self-righteous decrees and hidden agendas, stood as the ultimate obstacle to her ambitions. "And I have something they want," she continued, her voice dropping to a dangerous whisper. "Alpha fucking Blood!" Sly's eyes widened in comprehension as Azure revealed her trump card, the key to unlocking untold power and influence.

"But they want to hoard it, keep it locked away for their own purposes," Azure continued, her tone laced with disdain. "But I know its true potential. With enough of it, we could rival the Assembly itself." The plan had already begun to take shape in Azure's mind, a vision of rebellion and conquest. She spoke of the alliances and loyalty she has with some of the other purebloods within the territory and of a future where she stood unchallenged at the head of it all.

"And that's where you come in, Sly," Azure said, her voice switching back to soft but commanding. "I will be reaching out to our allies, to prepare them for what's to come. We'll need every vampire we can muster if we're going to succeed. I will be sending you to meet with them and discuss the plans I will give you soon." Sly nodded solemnly, his loyalty unwavering in the face of Azure's ambition. He knew the risks, the dangers that lay ahead, but he also knew that he would follow her into the abyss if she asked of him.

"And what about your new vamp puppy, Calathea?" he asked, his voice tinged with curiosity. A dangerous smile played across Azure's lips as she spoke of her plans for the younger vampire, her willingness to bend the rules to her own ends. "Calathea will be instrumental in our cause," she said, her eyes glittering with anticipation. "She's strong, loyal, and willing to do whatever it takes to see our vision realized." Sly's eyes widened in understanding as Azure revealed her intentions, his mind racing with the possibilities.

"Well, that's enough of that talk," she stated, suddenly changing her tone. "The thought of all of it has me feeling like I will drag you behind the bar and have my way with you. After all, you may be tough, but you're still my bitch. Ain't that right, Sly," she asked, her tone oozing with a depraved fervor she consumes as voraciously as she does human blood. "Anyways, so, what the fuck did you want?"

Sly began to share a piece of news that set Azure's mind ablaze with curiosity. A human, bold enough to walk into a vampire bar, purchasing blood for his lover, a newly turned vampire. Although it was a violation of vampire law, Azure has always remained indifferent towards those who defy the laws of their kind, as long as it didn't have any impact on her. However, her curiosity was sparked, her thoughts already swirling with possibilities. If this human, Kevin, was willing to defy convention for the sake of his lover, perhaps he could be persuaded to join her. She felt that if his love was that strong for her, then why not make the ultimate change for her? Azure would possibly see to it, either willingly or forcibly. If nothing else, a newly turned vampire could prove useful in the tumultuous days ahead.

With newfound purpose, Azure turned back towards the entrance of Plasmatic, her mind buzzing with plans and schemes. The night was alive with possibility, a storm gathering on the horizon, and Azure was ready to seize her rightful place at the head of it all. Sly trailed closely behind her, a bit more hesitant about what the future held, yet he remained steadfast in his determination to embrace whatever fate may befall them. But for now, first things first. Azure strode confidently towards the bar, determined to glean information from the bartender and owner. She was anxious to find out as much as she could about Kevin and his wife, and she was eager to do so without delay.

Chapter 16: An Undead Meet & Greet

The porch creaked under the weight of Azure and Calathea's steps, the night air thick with anticipation. Azure's hand hovered over the door, her knuckles pale against the wood as she prepared to knock. With a soft rap, the door swung open to reveal Kevin standing on the threshold. Azure's lips curled into a sly smile as she introduced herself and Calathea, her voice smooth and calm.

"Good evening, Kevin," Azure greeted him with a smile, her eyes dancing with mischief. "I hope we're not intruding." Kevin, expecting their presence, returned the greeting with a polite nod, his eyes flicking between Azure and Calathea. He stepped back slightly, leaving the door open in invitation, but Azure's sharp gaze stopped him in his tracks.

"Not so fast, Kevin," she teased, her voice laced with amusement. "You'll have to invite us in first, remember?" Kevin's eyes widened in realization as he quickly apologized, his cheeks flushing with embarrassment. He invited them in with a sheepish smile, his nerves evident in the way he fidgeted. Azure sighed softly, shaking her head in amusement as she stepped into the warmth of the house.

As they settled into their seats, Kevin offered them a drink before quickly retracting the offer, once again realizing his mistake. Calathea laughed softly at Kevin, her eyes twinkling with amusement as she glanced at Azure. Azure's attention was focused solely on Kevin, her gaze lingering on his features with a mixture of curiosity and intrigue.

As Kevin began to speak, Azure found herself oddly drawn to him. She listened intently as he spoke of his wife's plight, his words echoing with a sense of sadness and desperation. "I can easily understand the reason behind the enduring longevity of your relationship. Your apparent lack of fear is remarkable, considering you have managed to survive and still maintain this attitude." "Thank you," Kevin replied. Additionally, Azure added with a sly grin, "Not to mention, you're quite aesthetically pleasing." Calathea burst into laughter, unable to suppress it.

Could you enlighten me on the details such as when and how everything unfolded when she turned? Azure probed, eager to gather as much information as possible. As Kevin spoke, he cautiously shared snippets of information, hesitant to reveal too many details. But Kevin grew vague, in his explanations and Azure's curiosity turned into frustration. She probed him for more details, her patience wearing thin as he stumbled over his words.

"Come on now, Kevin," she chided gently, her voice tinged with impatience. "Surely you must remember more. Who was with you all? Where were you all at? What exactly happened leading up to it?" Kevin hesitated, his gaze shifting uncomfortably as he struggled to recall the events leading up to his wife's transformation. Azure pressed him for more, her determination shining brightly in her eyes. He then mentioned a neighbor they had encountered during their vacation in the Smokey Mountains.

Just then Azure's eyes widened as her interest in what Kevin was saying heightened. He explained to her that right before they left the cabin she was attacked by the neighbor's dog, who initially was going for his son Aaron. He tried to recall the name of the neighbor. "Don, Devin, Dale..." he uttered as he recited a list of names, attempting to recall the accurate one.

"God Damn Dean," Azure blurted out, cutting Kevin off. "Yes, Dean, that's it!" She knew of Dean, a powerful pureblood vampire with the ability to shapeshift. If he was involved in Christine's transformation, it could explain a great deal. "So, Dean didn't try to step come into the cabin with you all," Azure inquired. "No, he came to the door once and was invited in, but he declined. He for some odd reason kept looking around the room or the door for something.

Azure and Calathea exchanged looks, both seeming to know what the other was thinking. "Did there happen to be writings on the wall by the door," asked Azure. "Yes, now that you mention it, there was. There was writing along the back deck, back door, and front door. We couldn't make out what it said, but yes, there were writings,' Kevin replied. "Ah, the Sanguine writings," Calathea blurted out. "Those writings along the wall are probably the reason you all are still alive. With those carved or placed at an entrance, even with an invite, our kind aren't..." Calathea began to say before Azure abruptly cut her off so as to not expose such information. Kevin continued explaining the events that had taken place that week in the cabin. As Kevin continued to speak, Azure's mind whirled with plans and schemes. She saw an opportunity to use Christine to her advantage, to gain leverage over the Diaeta Assembly and secure her own position of power.

Azure's words began to dance on the edge of flirtation once again, her tone playful yet laced with a hint of genuine admiration. She couldn't help but marvel at Kevin's strength and resilience in taming Christine, a vampire born from the powerful blood of Dean. Something was captivating about the way he had weathered the storm, standing firm in the face of danger and uncertainty. As she spoke, Azure's eyes sparkled with mischief, her lips curving into a coy smile as she teased Kevin about his prowess.

In a moment of boldness, Azure ventured into more daring territory, hinting at the possibility of a deeper connection between them. She suggested the idea of Kevin joining Christine and becoming one of them, painting a picture of a trio bound together by their shared desires and ambitions. Her words carried a playful allure, tinged with a sense of excitement at the prospect of exploring new possibilities.

But Kevin's response was measured and cautious, his refusal tinged with a sense of longing. He was intrigued by Azure's offer, but his focus remained fixed on finding a way to restore Christine to her human form. Azure, typically not one to handle rejection gracefully, briefly felt a surge of anger. But she understood his priorities and respected his decision. Ultimately, she too possesses her own aspirations and longings. With a gentle smile, she reassured him that she would help Christine regardless, her words carrying a sense of determination and resolve.

Naturally, Azure was hesitant to disclose the secret to Kevin that would restore her human form. It wasn't due to its near impossibility, but because she had already devised a plan involving Christine. She intended to negotiate with Kevin, using Christine as a pawn in her scheme to seize control. However, she deemed it inappropriate to broach the subject at that particular moment.

As Azure and Kevin ascended the stairs toward the attic where Christine was confined, a subtle tension lingered in the air, noticeable yet unspoken. Azure's instincts told her to proceed cautiously, aware of the delicate balance of power within the confined space. With a glance back at Calathea, she urged her to remain seated, a silent acknowledgment of the potential volatility of the situation. Forcing a casual facade, Azure conveyed her confidence in Christine's awareness of their presence, a testament to the acute senses of a newborn vampire.

Yet, as they approached the attic, the tranquility was shattered by Christine's sudden outburst. Her voice tinged with anger and frustration through the attic door as she could be heard hurling insults and obscenities towards Azure. It was a stark reminder of the simmering resentment and hostility that lurked beneath the surface, threatening to erupt at any moment. In response, Azure merely arched an eyebrow, a knowing smirk playing on her lips as she exchanged a glance with Calathea as if to say "See, I told you so."

Meanwhile, Kevin's gaze switched back and forth between Azure and Calathea, a flicker of doubt clouding his expression. He couldn't shake the feeling of unease that gnawed at him, a nagging suspicion that there was more to Calathea's presence than meets the eye. Her malevolent grin only fueled his uncertainty, casting shadows of doubt upon her intentions. Caught in the crossfire of conflicting loyalties and hidden agendas, Kevin found himself teetering on the edge of trust.

As they entered the attic, Azure's eyes swept over the room, searching for any sign of movement. Christine's voice echoed from the shadows, her words dripping with disdain as she taunted Azure from her perch yet nowhere to be seen. Azure's lips curved into a sly smile as she addressed Christine, her voice dripping with amusement. "Christine, honey, aside from your unquenchable thirst, how are you doing?" Azure inquired, a blend of genuine concern and cynicism lacing her words.

In response, Christine's disembodied voice echoed from the depths of the attic, laced with more venomous intent and simmering rage. Her words further dripped with malice as she voiced her desire to extract pieces of Azure's body apart limb by limb, saving the head for last.

Unfazed by Christine's threats, Azure's lips turned into a sardonic smirk, her amusement dancing in the depths of her piercing gaze. With a casual ease that bordered on audacity, she engaged in a verbal sparring match with her caged adversary, their exchange laced with subtle jabs. Despite the gravity of the situation, Azure's irreverent banter remained a constant, a stark juxtaposition against the looming specter of danger. Azure was fully cognizant of the underlying purpose behind her sassy reply to Christine, as they both still possessed feminine characteristics.

Then, as if choreographed by some unseen force, Christine descended from the shadows with a fluidity that bordered on the supernatural. Her movements were sinuous and predatory, a silent reminder of the primal instincts that lurked beneath her veneer of civility. Azure met her gaze unflinchingly, her own demeanor a mixture of defiance and curiosity. With a mocking jest, she teased Christine with the prospect of a daring escape, their words a delicate dance of power and manipulation.

"Why haven't you managed to break free if you're so big and bad? It seems you're incapable, am I right?"

Amid their tense standoff, Azure took a step closer to Christine, their eyes locked in a silent battle of wills. There was a fleeting moment of vulnerability in Christine's gaze, a flicker of longing masked by a facade of resignation. Sensing her inner turmoil, Azure extended a silent offer of liberation, a glimmer of hope amidst the shadows of confinement. Silence followed their encounter, not a single word spoken between them, at least not audible to a human ear. Yet, in that fleeting moment, both Azure and Christine shared an unspoken bond of understanding and admiration for each other.

As Azure turned to exit the attic, Christine retreated into the shadows once more, her form disappearing into the darkness like a wraith vanishing into the night. Perplexed by the events that had unfolded, Kevin turned to Christine with a sorrowful gaze and declared, "I will do whatever it takes Christine to bring you back, I love you." To Kevin's surprise, Christine responded with words and a voice that evoked memories of her former self, "I love you too Kevin."

As they made their way back downstairs, Azure's mind raced with possibilities. She knew she had to tread carefully to navigate the delicate web of alliances and even the possibility of rivalries that surrounded her there. Each of the trio had their own individual motives and personal requirements that they prioritized above all else. Azure's curiosity was still piqued as she prepared to leave, she couldn't help but inquire of Kevin, "Has your young son, Aaron, taken the COVID vaccination yet?" Perplexed by Azure's logic behind the inquiry, he nodded his head with a brief confirmation. "That's fantastic news. It appears that we may be able to come to an ideal agreement after all," she responded.

As they stepped out into the night, Azure turned to Kevin with a smile, her eyes sparkling with mischief. "I shall return very soon. I have a few things to put into motion first that shouldn't take long at all. But once I'm done, I will take her with me for a while. You of course or welcome at any time. You will be safe with her as long as I'm around." As she made her way to the vehicle, she abruptly spun on her heels, adding, "By the way, it may be worthwhile to reconsider my initial proposal. It's not so bad here on the other side as you think, handsome!" Azure was not one to back down from a challenge, especially when it came to achieving her goals. She knew what she wanted, a chair, or the only chair at the Diaeta Assembly table. Accompanied by Christine, who held immense potential, her desire for power became even more insatiable.

Chapter 17: Powers Revealed

The laughter of children playing in the street filled the air, mingling with the gentle rustle of leaves in the breeze. Among them, young Aaron stood, his shoulders slumped with the weight of his torment. The air crackled with tension as he faced off against his bully, the weight of his emotions heavy in his chest.

The bully, a towering figure among his peers, taunted Aaron mercilessly, his words like daggers aimed at the boy's heart. "Hey loser, where's your mommy?" the bully jeered, his voice dripping with malice. "Oh wait, that's right, she left you because you're nothing but a pathetic crybaby. She's not even your real mommy, so of course she left!"

With each cruel word, Aaron's resolve crumbled, his eyes brimming with unshed tears. He tried to ignore the bully's taunts, to block out the laughter of the other children, but it was no use. The pain cut deep, carving a wound in his young heart that seemed impossible to heal. The bully's words echoed in his mind, a constant reminder of the pain he had endured.

As the bully shoved him to the ground, Aaron felt his world spin out of control. With watery eyes, he lifted himself back to his feet and began the walk home, the echoes of the taunts ringing in his ears. With each stride toward his home, it seemed as though time itself was decelerating, each pace laced with defeat.

But as he approached his house, a strange sensation washed over him. His gaze fell upon two women leaving his house, their presence like a ripple in the fabric of reality. Unbeknownst to Aaron, one of these women, Azure, held secrets far beyond his comprehension. They had been visiting his father, Kevin, to help him with a family crisis that Aaron could scarcely begin to understand. And yet, as their eyes met, a connection sparked between them.

With a heavy heart, Aaron stepped onto his front porch, his eyes still glistening with unshed tears. Kevin, who had been standing by the door already seeing out Azure and Calathea, noticed his son's distress and rushed to his side, concern etched on his face. "What's wrong dude," Kevin asked, his voice laced with worry.

In a voice choked with emotion, Aaron recounted his encounter with the bully, his words tumbling out in a rush. Kevin's jaw clenched with anger as he listened. "Well, I want you to listen to me and listen to me right now! We don't run away from our problems Aaron," Kevin said, his voice firm. "We face them head-on, and we don't stop until we figure them out and find a solution to them!"

While standing in place, Kevin remained motionless, obstructing the doorway and preventing Aaron from entering. Aaron immediately recognized the implications of this. His dad said what he said. That means not later but handle it right then. With a determined nod, Aaron wiped away his tears and squared his shoulders, a newfound resolve burning bright in his eyes. He knew what he had to do.

Returning to the scene of his humiliation, Aaron felt a surge of confidence coursing through his veins. The other children watched in awe as he approached the bully, their whispers fading into the background as Aaron's gaze locked with his tormentor's. As the bully caught sight of him drawing near, he abruptly halted his actions and commenced ridiculing Aaron with greater intensity, eventually delivering a final forceful shove.

As Aaron stood there, his father's wise words echoed in his mind, "You don't run from your problems, you figure out a way to overcome them!" And then, with a strength he didn't know he possessed, he extended his arms toward the bully, sending him flying back with an unseen force. Although it appeared that Aaron had pushed him, there was no physical contact between them leaving Aaron perplexed.

As the bully scrambled to his feet, confusion etched on his face, Aaron stood tall, his mood unshakable. Filled with fury, once more the bully advanced towards Aaron, driven by revenge for retribution. Again, Aaron stretched out his arms, this time with increased conviction, holding them aloft. As he did so, his opponent was once again propelled backward onto the ground but pushed even further back than the unexpected strength from the first encounter.

As the bully scrambled to his feet, confusion etched on his face. With a final glance back at Aaron, that of defeat, the bully turned and walked away. As he did so the cheers of his fickle peers rang out in Aaron's ears. As he stood there receiving high-fives and pats on the back, he still didn't understand what had just taken place, he just knew that it felt right.

But then, he began to sense that unsettling feeling, much like the one he had experienced earlier when he was making his way back home. He experienced the identical sensation as when he faced Dean at the cabin years ago. As he shifted his gaze to the street, he caught sight of the woman who had recently departed from his home sitting there in her car. Her look conveyed a sense of awe and curiosity as she had been watching the whole time.

As Aaron made his way home, a sense of unease gnawed in his mind. He couldn't shake the feeling that something had changed within him, something powerful and undeniable. Meanwhile, Kevin had remained on the front steps of the porch, catching the echoes of jubilation emanating from the nearby children.

"So, what the hell just happened," Kevin inquired as he moved to the side, letting Aaron into the house. "I figured it out and took care of it," Aaron responded with a casual and understated tone before heading to the kitchen in search of a quick bite. With a quizzical lift of his eyebrow, Kevin couldn't help but let out a small smile, thinking to himself, "Naturally, he solved it. He is my offspring, after all. I had no doubt he would."

Kevin's pride in his son was short-lived as just then the bully's father arrived, anger etched on his face as he stood on the porch. "Excuse me, are you Aaron's dad," he asked. He bore a resemblance to his son, both in looks and physique. It was as if he were an older version of his child; Hence, he was also slightly larger than Kevin.

"I sure am, what's up," Kevin replied, looking at him directly in his eyes. "Well, your son or you or whoever owes my son a new pair of eyeglasses. I was told your son flung them to the ground," he exclaimed. Kevin, looking the man up and down with a quick glance replied, "Look at me and you. Now picture your son and my son standing in front of each other the same way. One would think if your son had his eyeglasses knocked off, maybe it was because he did something causing him to underestimate who was in front of him. So, my suggestion is, don't start no shit it won't be no shit!" Kevin remained completely still, not a single muscle twitching nor refusing to back down. His words were a defiant challenge to the man before him. And as the bully's father slunk away, defeated, Kevin couldn't help but think, "Like father like son I suppose."

As he closed the door behind him, Kevin's gaze fell upon Aaron, who stood just a few feet away, his expression a mixture of confusion and sadness. With a heavy sigh, Aaron confided in his father, the words tumbling out. He missed his stepmother, Christine, he missed her laughter and her love, and he longed for the day when she would return to normal.

Kevin's heart broke at his son's words, the pain etched in his eyes mirroring Aaron's own. He knew that Christine weighed heavily on them both, a constant reminder of the darkness that lurked in their lives. Even as they grappled with their grief, Kevin vowed to his son that they would find a way to bring Christine back to them, to restore her to the woman she once was.

But for now, all Kevin could do was hold his son close, his heart heavy with the weight of their shared sorrow. At that instant, while standing there in the embrace of each other, they were certain that it would eventually regain its former essence. And within that moment of silence, a voice echoed through the home. "Good job, Aaron! Good job, son!" The words originated from a section of the home that contained the cherished being, one who held a special place, in their Hearts.

Chapter 18: Breaking News!

―――――――――――◆●◆―――――――――――

Dave sat in his home office, the glow of the computer screen casting a pale light across his features as he sifted through his emails one last time before bed. His fingers hovered over the keyboard, his mind already halfway drifting into a state of relaxation. The soft hum of the monitor fills the air as he sifts through the last remnants of the day's correspondence. His weary eyes scan each email, searching for any urgent messages that may have slipped through the cracks.

In the quiet solitude of his home office, Dave's thoughts drift to the early morning ahead. As the anchor of the 5 am news broadcast, he knows that sleep will elude him for a few more hours yet. With a sigh, he resigns himself to the familiar routine of late-night emails and last-minute preparations.

Just as he begins to settle into his last tasks for the night, the door opens, and a figure appears in the doorway. It's his wife, Nancy, her silhouette softened by the gentle light streaming in from the hallway. A warm smile graces her lips as she bids him goodnight. Dave returns the kiss with an embrace. "I'll be to bed soon," his voice a soft murmur. With a final glance, Nancy retreats to the sanctuary of their bedroom, leaving Dave alone with his thoughts once more.

Turning back to his computer, Dave reaches for his cup of tea, the fragrant steam rising in delicate tendrils. The soothing aroma fills the room. As the minutes slip by, Dave loses himself in the rhythmic clicking of the keyboard and the soft glow of the screen casting a halo around the room. But then, amidst the mundane messages and spam, he stumbled upon an email that sent a chill down his spine. Dave's heart raced as he sat in front of his computer in stone silence, the glow of the screen illuminating was the only loud presence in the room.

The email was from Gail Preston, the missing scientist. Opening it and seeing her name felt like a bolt from the blue, shaking him to his core. His hands trembled as he read the contents, The mere utterance of each syllable paralyzes him with a surge of fear. Gail had been missing for over two years, her disappearance shrouded in mystery and speculation. Dave's hands trembled more and more as he scrolled, his eyes scanning the words in disbelief.

The revelation about the COVID-19 vaccine and its sinister manipulation by powerful forces was enough to make his blood run cold. The implications of what he was reading were staggering—secret societies, vampires, and a plot to weaponize the vaccine for nefarious purposes. Dave's mind reeled with the enormity of it all, struggling to comprehend the depths of the conspiracy.

Summoning his wife Nancy to his side, Dave shared the contents of the email, the gravity of the situation weighing heavily upon them both. Nancy's eyes widened in shock as she began to read, her hand flying to her mouth in disbelief. Together, they poured over the details of Gail's message and its content files, their minds racing with fear and uncertainty.

As they delve deeper into the contents of the email, his heart quickens with each revelation. The words on the screen paint a picture of deception and betrayal on a global scale. The COVID-19 vaccine, held as a lifesaver in the fight against the pandemic, has been tainted by an evil agenda.

The file and the email fully detail how an additional spiked protein was intentionally introduced into the vaccine, and covertly inserted into doses distributed worldwide, particularly targeting the US. What's even more disturbing is that this nefarious act was orchestrated by high-ranking government officials, influential pharmaceutical lobbyists, a few of the very creators of the vaccine, and, shockingly, a society of governing vampires.

The concept of vampires living amongst them all is something he had dismissed as mere folklore, yet here it is laid bare before him. The email unveils the motive behind the vaccine's contamination: the young humans inoculated with this tainted vaccine become unwitting targets for vampires, their blood infused with a potent allure that makes them irresistible prey.

Yet, amidst the darkness, a glimmer of hope emerges. Gail's email illuminates the extraordinary potential latent within Generation Alpha, the young individuals unwittingly endowed with this altered DNA. The spiked protein not only integrates with their genetic code but enhances their physical and sensory capabilities, granting them powers beyond imagination. These abilities are not instant but mature with the passage of time.

Dave's mind reels with the implication of the email. The fate of humanity hangs in the balance, teetering on the brink of an unprecedented crisis. But one thing seems clear; The Alpha Generation may hold the key to salvation. With their newfound abilities and innate ability to detect vampires, they may be humanity's only hope against the undead, If these findings are to be true.

Gail's plea to Dave carries the weight of desperation and urgency. As he reads her words, he can almost feel the fear and helplessness emanating from the screen. She trusts him implicitly, knowing that as a respected news anchor and a friend, he possesses the influence and platform needed to expose the truth to the world. Dave's heart clenches at the thought of Gail's captivity, her voice silenced by unseen powerful forces.

Her message is a lifeline thrown into the darkness; Gail's words convey not only the gravity of the situation but also the perilous dangers she faces. Threatened by both vampires and government agents, she exists in a precarious limbo, teetering on the edge of oblivion. As Dave absorbs Gail's final instructions, a surge of determination courses through him. He vows to honor her wishes and to safeguard her identity at all costs.

As Dave reassures Nancy, his mind buzzes with the weight of responsibility. He knows sleep won't come easy tonight, not when the fate of countless lives hangs in the balance. With another goodnight kiss from Nancy, he feels a surge of determination. Nancy's worries linger in the air as she retires to bed, a silent testament to the gravity of the situation.

Alone in his home office, Dave's fingers dance across the keys of his phone, dialing numbers with a sense of urgency. Each call is a lifeline and a crucial link in the chain of verification. He speaks to a few sources, experts, and contacts, piecing together the puzzle of Gail's revelation. The weight of each conversation presses down on him, a reminder of the stakes at hand.

In the quiet hours of the night, Dave's determination remains unyielding. His pursuit of truth is relentless, driving him forward even as exhaustion threatens to pull him under. With each call, he inches closer to unraveling the web of deception that shrouds Gail's message. As dawn approaches, Dave knows that his mission has only just begun.

Sitting in front of the camera the next morning, the studio lights cast long shadows across Dave's face, masking the turmoil brewing beneath the surface. As the countdown begins, tension crackles in the air, a silent chorus of nerves and apprehension. Dave's pulse quickens, his heart hammering in his chest. With each passing number from 10 to one from the cameraman, the gravity of the moment intensifies, the weight of his words poised to reshape the very fabric of reality.

Finally, as the countdown reaches its crescendo, Dave's voice cuts through the silence like a clarion call. "Well, good morning, Nashville! This is Channel 6 News, your leading source of current News. I'm Dave Hall. We began today with breaking news ...."

About the Author

The Author, C.M. James is a fresh face in the literature scene. Having recently entered the world of being an author, he is determined to make his mark in the novel world. But don't let his newness fool you - C.M. James is a seasoned wordsmith, with a natural talent for expressing his thoughts and ideas through written word and storytelling. His unique outlook adds a refreshing and captivating element to his writing, making it stand out among the rest. In his works, C.M. James seamlessly weaves together elements of intrigue, mystery, suspense, and drama. But that's not all - he also adds a generous dose of thought-provoking themes and unexpected twists to keep readers on their toes.

As a new author, C.M. James is ready to prove himself to be a master storyteller with a unique style. His writing is a perfect blend of talent, skill, and passion, making it impossible to put down once you start reading. With each new work, he continues to establish himself as a force to be reckoned with in the world of literature, and his future works are eagerly anticipated by his readers.

The individual, C.M James is just a well-rounded person who has faced many challenges and triumphs throughout his life.
This diverse range of experiences has not only shaped C.M. as a person but has also greatly influenced his writing style. With his ability to adapt to various situations, he can bring a unique and relatable perspective to his writing. Whether it's through his

characters or the themes he explores, there is always something that readers can connect with. Moreover, C.M.'s experiences have also allowed him to relate to people from all walks of life. This understanding and empathy shine through in his writing, making it all the more impactful. He aspires for his readers to become lifelong readers of his writings and delight in all that they may bring.

Made in the USA
Columbia, SC
27 May 2024